20

LIFE
ON THE
GREAT LAKES

GREAT LAKES BOOKS

A complete listing of the books in this series can be found at the back of this volume.

Philip P. Mason, Editor
Walter P. Reuther Library, Wayne State University

Dr. Charles K. Hyde, Associate Editor
Department of History, Wayne State University

Advisory Editors

Photo courtesy of Robert Packo-Toledo.

LIFE
ON THE
GREAT LAKES

A WHEELSMAN'S STORY

Fred W. Dutton

Edited by
William Donohue Ellis

Wayne State University Press   Detroit
The Great Lakes Historical Society

Manufactured in the United States of America

95 94 93 92 91   5 4 3 2 1

Library of Congress Cataloging-in-Publication Data

Dutton, Fred W.
    Life on the Great Lakes : a wheelsman's story / Fred W. Dutton ; edited by William Donohue Ellis.
        p.   cm. —(Great Lakes books)
    "Great Lakes Historical Society."
    ISBN 0-8143-2260-3 (alk. paper). —ISBN 0-8143-2261-1 (pbk. : alk. paper)
    1. Seafaring life—Great Lakes—History—20th century. 2. Great Lakes—Social life and customs. 3. Great Lakes—Description and travel. 4. Dutton, Fred W. 5. Merchant seamen—Great Lakes—Biography. 6. Ore carriers—History—20th century. I. Ellis, William Donohue. II. Great Lakes Historical Society. III. Title. IV. Series.
F551.D88 1991
917.704'33—dc20   90-49241
                                                 CIP

William Donohue Ellis is also editor of *Inland Seas*® and author of *Land of the Inland Seas, The Bounty Lands Trilogy,* and *The Ordinance of 1787.*

The book was designed by Mary Primeau.

To my shipmates . . . whom I owe for countless hours of deep-drunk enjoyment in their society. Good fellows, with one or two exceptions, of good humor, intelligent, philosophers all, skilled seamen, possessing an inexhaustible store of know-how, who have an amazing capacity for jumping into an emergency and doing the right thing without any fuss. These are the men who man the Great Lakes vessels, carrying at this writing the greatest flow of commerce anywhere in the world.

CONTENTS

CONTENTS

EDITOR'S INTRODUCTION

In the days when a stern gale sweetened the pilothouse with a fragrance of bunker coal smoke and navigation through night fog in the narrows was by holding the breath to listen sharp for traffic, few seamen wrote down the work-a-day operations, much less the character of the crew.

Fred Dutton did.

He thereby gave us, concentrated in a single volume, detail which otherwise would need to be strained in fragments from a hundred sources.

Since it is a first-person chronicle, we hear errant iron ore chunks bouncing off the pilothouse at loading docks and strain our eyes to glimpse marine markers through blizzards while running for the lee of islands.

This work was first published serially in *Inland Seas*® beginning in the Fall 1981 issue. A demand developed to have the story available in a single volume. Mr. Dutton's manuscript contains vessel operation detail usually only available in the dialogue of a passing generation of very elderly sailors. Now it is preserved here for future generations.

Howard H. Baxter and Timothy J. Runyan, both long-time officers and trustees of the Great Lakes Historical Society, encouraged the editing of the series into a book manuscript. Wayne State University Press took over from there, giving it the beautiful book production for which they are noted. Anne M. G. Adamus and Kathryn Wildfong, editors of the Press, managed publication.

If a working boat is not in the files of Jerry Metzler of Lakewood, Ohio, it is a ghost ship. He has built and constantly maintains an enormous archival data collection on Great Lakes vessels. He checked every vessel in this manuscript against his data and corrected a few where Fred Dutton had either rounded off the numbers or had forgotten a detail.

Fred Dutton's daughter, Susan (Mrs. Jerry King), of Denver, Colorado, has been interested and helpful.

My colleagues Nancy A. Schneider and Alan W. Sweigert, both editors of *Inland Seas*®, worked on this manuscript. Sweigert, veteran chronicler of the lakes, shot many of the photographs to illustrate the book.

Martha Long, business manager of the Great Lakes Historical Society, sought out photos from the Society's museum collection.

Readers of this book might like to know more about Fred Dutton. Thomas A. ("Andy") Sykora, Great Lakes Historical Society trustee and secretary, was a close friend of his, and at my request he prepared the following picture of Fred Dutton, who died in 1980.

His was a natural friendship that lasted over twenty years.

Shortly after the founding of the Great Lakes Historical

Society on May 11, 1944, word spread about the reasons for the Society's existence along with its ambitious goal of preserving Great Lakes maritime history. One interesting fellow became intensely curious and contacted Clarence S. Metcalf, my grandfather, one of the founders, who welcomed him and his love of the old lake boats. This new charter member had sailed the lakes and preserved the memory of the vessels he had sailed by photographing them and scores of other boats. Years later, after he had become a railroad lawyer, he began writing about his experiences.

Frederick W. Dutton later became the valued treasurer of the Society, giving it stability.

Long after Fred Dutton became a lawyer, he kept a hand on a ship's wheel, each summer arranging with steamship companies to sail relief wheelsman during his vacation. One summer in 1950 while I struggled up a ladder to be deckhand aboard the venerable old steamer *Colonel*, I was greeted on deck by wheelsman Fred Dutton, who had just hauled my gear aboard. We crewed together for a brief period before Fred returned to the beach and to his paneled office.

Over the years we swapped pictures and Great Lakes gossip. Still later, I went to work for the operations department of a steamship company located in the same building as his paneled office, so our friendship endured.

In 1964 Fred retired from the law department of the Chesapeake & Ohio Railway Company, and, as planned, he and his wife and daughter, Susan, moved to Denver, Colorado.

Fred had also been very active in the Cleveland Power Squadron. An expert on weather forecasting, he instructed the squadron weather classes for years and continued even after his move to Denver. His annual Christmas card was a picture of a lakes freighter.

A long period of failing health preceded his death on August 6, 1980.

Fred Dutton's family presented Sykora with Dutton's personal photo collection, which Sykora generously lent us. Selections appear in this book.

Dutton's memories give an unusual view of Great Lakes America from the pilothouse. I extend my personal invitation for the reader to get behind the wheel.

CHAPTER I

INITIATION

I was vaguely scared.

I was walking along the C.&P. ore dock at Cleveland, Ohio, and there was the *Charlotte Graveraet Breitung* alongside me, a wall of black steel rising way up above my head, exhaling steam. Though she was under five thousand gross tons, she looked like a continent. She was owned by Juliet-Graveraet Steamship Company, Cleveland.

This was my first day and my first ship. Maybe my last. I was filled with doubts and dismay. This was 1916, and I was 16. What did I know about being a deckhand?

A hundred questions crowded me. How would I know what my duties were? How would I know where my bunk was? The men would probably make fun of my ignorance and mistakes. How would I know when and where to get my pay? Did I have the right clothes? I might get sick. I might fall off the dock when handling the cables. I might get off to a bad start with the first mate.

Editor's note: Young Dutton's eleventh-hour shakes were not without reason. Unlike other young first-time deckhands, he already knew enough about vessels to know some hazards of ore boats and mates.

His father worked for an iron ore company in Marquette, entitling his family to one trip per year on an ore boat. So he had seen plenty of hazards, and participated in some.

One year, for example, when he was only seven, the family was riding the Powell Stackhouse, owned by M. A. Hanna Company. The vessel was unloading coal. Young Dutton and his brother went out on deck to watch. He recalls what happened.

As we walked aft, the great swinging clamshell buckets seemed to hurtle right at me, but they always stopped their swing and dropped out of sight in the hold.

Returning forward, my older brother and I ran the deck. Leading the way, I tore up the middle of the deck like a wild Indian. All thirty hatches were open, with the coal filling most of them right up to the deck. Jumping from deck to coal-filled hatch to deck again was wonderful fun!

All of a sudden I disappeared from sight. A thin scream must have been heard. Scared witless, my brother stopped in his headlong course and looked over the coaming of the next hatch. It was three-fourths empty, and he saw me lying on a sloping bank of coal twenty feet below. He joined in my screaming.

The first mate came running; sailors gathered about. When the mate saw me in the hold, he ran over and climbed through the small hatch near the winches and rapidly down the iron ladder into the cargo hold. Reaching bottom, he ran over and climbed up the coal, stumbling and slipping as the lumps rolled under his feet. Picking me up, after feeling quickly for broken bones, and holding me in one arm, he climbed the ladder one-handed. The second mate pulled me through the small hatch; the first mate carried me into the passenger quarters and laid me down on my bed.

Self-unloader in the iron inferno.

My screaming subsided to a whimper, as the first mate, livid with anger, gave me a tongue lashing I will never forget. "Don't you ever forget for an instant that the first rule, and the last, on a steamboat is be goddam careful! You are lucky. On a steamboat you seldom get a second chance!"

Editor's note: As a former passenger on steamers, Dutton knew that he had enjoyed a privileged, protected view of the life. But now, as he approached the Breitung *as a deckhand, he knew he had no such privileges.*

But I finally told myself: You asked for it. You badgered your father to let you go decking. Now go ahead and show him.

You can't go back home now.

I climbed up the long ladder, suitcase in one hand—a difficult thing to do. I had a moment's fear of falling off but finally made it and jumped down onto the steel deck.

There was no one around, though I saw two or three men up near the forward cabins. I felt like a stranger and a fool. I saw a man coming around the corner of the after cabin.

He spoke. "You the new deckhand?"

"Yes, sir, I guess I am."

"Don't call me sir. I'm only the watchman. Come along, I'll show you where your room is at." He led aft alongside the cabin. Stopping just abaft the boiler house, he pushed open a door. "You can put your stuff in there, Slim. I guess you get that lower berth."

I thanked the watchman. Two other very young men were sitting on the lower berth.

"Hello," one of them said. "I guess this is your bunk." They both got up and stepped aside for me. Uncertainly, I put my suitcase down. I wanted to ask questions but held back. One of them said, "My name's Roy—Roy Ferguson."

The other followed: "Jim Wilson." We shook hands.

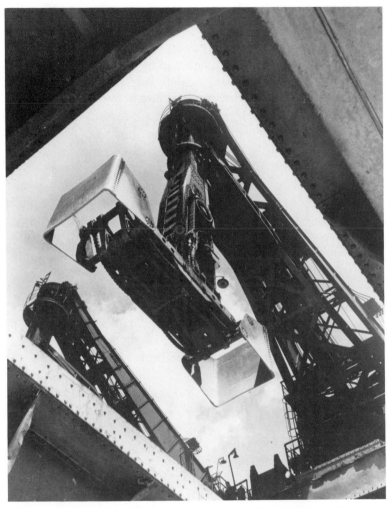

The jaws of the Hulett. (Photo courtesy of the McDowell-Wellman Companies.)

"This your first time?" asked Roy.

"Yes. Feels kind of strange."

"Here, too. Jim and I only been on this boat for two trips. You'll get the hang of it." They told me to put my grip under the bunk and showed me which was my drawer in the miniature dresser in the corner. They helped me clean out the last occupant's least-treasured possessions, including work gloves so petrified in paint that they were permanent fists. Eyeing the blue sheets appliquéd with coal-dust handprints, I felt a little homesick.

Jim said, "You can take your linen with you to supper and give it to the porter; he'll give you clean. And your towel." He indicated by the washbowl a roller towel which was a display panel for samples of iron ore, deck paint, and machine oil.

Roy Ferguson was a short, stocky kid with a mop of unruly curly hair and Ireland all over his face. Jim Wilson was taller, slight, fair-skinned, and sober-faced.

There was a sudden clangor of a bell, and immediately another young man in a cook's apron stuck his head in the door, ringing a brass handbell. "Come and get it!"

"Better wash up quick," Roy advised.

I did. Grabbing the bed linen and the multicolored towel, I followed them.

The mess room was only next door, so we were the first in. I sat on a stool next to Roy. A big chap wearing an apron and a chef's hat leaned against the door frame, looking us over gravely. "You again! I only fed you about an hour ago. The company's going broke feeding you."

He brought in a steaming platter.

A fireman and a coal passer came in without speaking.

There was evidence they had tried to wash up. Coal dust ringed their bloodshot eyes and their ears and necks. Their hands were black. The two started stoking their plates with great chunks of the meat and potatoes and cabbage.

My hunger finally overcame my curiosity, and I, too, began to eat.

When we three returned to our room, I asked, "When do we go to work?"

Roy said, "Soon enough. But the first mate gives us a lot of time off when we have to work at night."

"Do we work at night, too?"

Roy answered, "You don't think they tie the ship up at night, do you?" But he explained we only had to handle lines on the dock when in port or going through the Soo. "And once in a while haul groceries aboard, and maybe pull the hatches or stow the anchor chain. But there isn't much to do tonight, only finish putting on the hatch covers. They'll rinse her down in the morning."

I held back my other questions but kept my ears open.

Jim was sound asleep in his bunk, his snores filling the room, and soon Roy, too, was as good as dead. I felt lonesome.

I was wondering what to do next, when a voice blasted through the snoring, "Come on, deckaroos! Out on the dock."

Jim and Roy sprang out of their bunks as if bitten. I followed. Each grabbed up an old, dirty pair of canvas gloves.

"Got any gloves, Fred?"

"Yeah," I answered, and I pulled out my suitcase to get them. I followed them out on deck.

Roy started down the ladder, but Jim said, "You don't

have to go down. She'll just move down the dock, then we'll cast off, and they don't need three men for that."

I was left standing by the rail, feeling in the way. Another sailor ran up and grabbed the ladder.

"Here, Slim, help with this." The ladder was about twenty feet long, with oak rails and steel rungs. My arms felt pulled out of their sockets.

"Hold on now. Don't let it slip." He took a turn with a line around the ladder. "All right now, you can ease off."

I was shaking with the effort and leaned against the rail. The winches were clattering, the steel cables leading to the dock snapped taut. Slowly the steamer moved astern along the dock.

A voice from the bridge, far forward, yelled out, "Let go the after cable!" The sailor at the rail gestured to another working the winch steam valves. The winch reversed with a bang. The cable slacked. The sailor frantically beckoned to the winch man. "Stick out! Stick out!" Suddenly he held up his hand. The winch stopped; steam squealed around the cylinders.

"Throw it off!" the second mate yelled to Jim down on the dock. I saw Jim lift the cable loop off the bollard and let it go. I wondered for a moment how Jim was going to get back on board.

The second mate started a winding motion with his hand. The winch gave forth another bang and clattered louder as the cable came in through the chock. Jim was running toward the forward end of the ship along the dock. The ship was leaving!

The second mate grabbed my arm and hollered in my ear, "Get forward and help with that forward ladder." I ran forward. Just aft of the fo'c'sle, they were putting another ladder down. The ship trembled as the engines began turning over. Reaching the forward end, I saw Roy and Jim

Steam dock winch. (Alan W. Sweigert photo.)

climbing the ladder while the ship's stern was already swinging out. But Roy and Jim made it over the rail, and we all
heaved the ladder up on deck.

"Get away from that cable!" someone yelled at me. I

backed away from the cable stretching from the winch to the rail.

"You'll get killed if that cable parts."

A voice yelled for me to go aft again and help with the other ladder.

The ship made an angle of ninety degrees with the dock now, when a blast from the whistle startled me. Voices called somewhere up forward, followed by the bang and rattle of the forward winch, and soon I noticed that the steamer was backing away from the dock. The engines stopped for a minute, then started again, shaking the ship throughout. Slowly she came around, heading for the harbor entrance. We were under way.

"All right, fellows, get a move on." It was the second mate. "Get these hatches on her now."

I had seen it done many times before when I was a passenger, but now it was all different. Jim was saying, "You handle the dolly bar this time. It's more dangerous to work with the bridle. You can do it another time, when it's daylight. If you ever fell down the hold, you'd be a dead duck. Here, first you put the dolly bar in the socket at the rail—like this—then step clear of the cable, *outside* the bight. Never inside. If anything ever let go, you want to be in the clear. Don't forget it!"

Jim ran over and helped Roy pull the light steel cable out until they could put the rings of the bridle around the buttons on the hatch cover. He looked to see that everything was clear and no one was in the way, then he raised his hand and made the same winding motion the second mate used.

I looked toward the winch that pulled the hatch covers on. The watchman at the winch opened the steam valve, the cable tightened. Boom, boom, boom—the telescoping steel hatch covers slid along the hatch coamings until they stopped suddenly with a bang that echoed through the empty vessel. At the same instant, Jim dropped his hand in a signal to the winch operator, who yanked the reverse lever and shut off the steam. Jim and Roy snatched the rings of the bridle off the buttons and raced to the next hatch, Jim yelling, "All right, Slim, grab that dolly bar and run it up to the next hatch!"

In half an hour the hatches were closed, the pins were in, and we went aft to our room.

In all that slam-bang confusion, there had been a tremendously precise system. I wondered if I would learn it.

Once outside the harbor, the wind played a tune in the rigging, and a small chop of sea running made the ship roll. We stopped in the mess room for coffee and a sandwich. I was beginning to feel I wanted to be a part of this crew, a part of this ship. But I had a long way to go.

By eleven o'clock, all of us were so tired that we turned in, and that night I knew that special feeling of going to sleep on a steamship, lulled by the beat of the engines, very pronounced back there in the stern. Before, as a passenger, I had always slept in the forward end, several hundred feet from the engines.

The next thing I knew, I was awakened by the steamer's whistle, very loud, right overhead. The room was located but a few feet aft of the smokestack, and the whistle was up there on the stack. Three blasts. Half awake, I wondered why three blasts. Then it dawned on me. Fog. Each minute, the whistle let go shuddering blasts. You could hardly think. I dropped off to sleep again, but a minute later the roar woke me. I sat up. Roy and Jim were oblivious. But I couldn't sleep. The homesickness crept over me again.

In the gray light of morning, I saw the fog through the

screen door, swirling past, even coming in the door. You could hardly see the bulwarks six feet beyond the door. The muted tremor of the ship indicated engines turning, dead slow.

I dressed, wondering what my mother would think if she knew my pajamas were still folded in my grip. Working a steamboat, you sleep in your shorts, ready to get on deck quickly.

SUNDAY SAILING

Apparently deckhand duty on Sunday is eating and sleeping. The breakfast bell exploded. Breakfast was ham and eggs, cereal, milk, oranges, toast, coffee—and we three had seconds.

Then we stretched out in our bunks again and fell asleep.

The fog was thinning out. The big whistle only blew now when we met another freighter. The "*Charletty Cravanette,*" as the sailors affectionately called the *Breitung,* was smoothly steaming up the Detroit River.

"Hey," I asked, "when do we go to work?"

Roy opened his eyes in disgust. "On Sunday? Not unless we're in port. Sunday is the day of rest."

"I thought you said we'd rinse down the deck."

"Not this time." Roy sat up, rubbing his head. "The watchman and the deck watch did that this morning."

"Why do they have to work, when we don't?"

"Those guys stand watches—six hours on, six off. They don't have Sunday off, or any other day."

I asked why anyone would want watch duty.

"They like it all right," Jim put in, awake now. "They get more money—forty-five a month. And when they are off watch they don't ever have to work. The deckhands work

Fred Dutton (*right*) with Andy Sykora. (Photo courtesy of the Dutton Collection.)

all day, and if we are in port we might work all night, too. Somebody's got to handle the lines; that's us."

The door opened, and the watchman stuck his head in. "Hey, you, Slim. Go up to the mate's room. He wants you."

"Where is the mate's room?"

"Forward. First door in the starboard hallway."

I knocked on the first door, expecting the mate to have a job for me.

"Come in. Good morning." The first mate greeted me. Instantly I liked the man. "Here." He had a large printed form spread out on the desk. Handing me a pencil, he indicated the place to sign the articles, an ancient rule of the sea. I signed. "Now you're signed up for the voyage. Do your work and you'll get along fine." He eyed my slight frame. "This ought to put some meat on you."

Leaving, I met Captain Buchanan, who welcomed me aboard.

When I returned to the deckhands' room, I found Roy and Jim asleep again. We all slept until dinner. I gorged myself, but I never seemed to get enough.

After supper we played rummy, got a sandwich and a piece of cake in the mess room, and turned in by nine o'clock.

Why would a sailor need all this food and sleep?

I was to find out.

We chipped paint and rust interminably. We spent days on end painting the cabins, the bulwarks, the cargo hold, the deck.

I was introduced to the joys of soogeying. Handling iron ore or coal, each time they are in port, these steamships are covered with dirt and grime. The condition is not permitted to last. The answer is soogey. No sooner do boats leave port than the rinsing down begins, clearing the decks of all loose ore or coal. The high-pressure hose scours thoroughly. The cabins are soogeyed every two or three trips. Water is heated by putting the bucket under the end of a steam pipe until it boils. With a generous portion of gold dust added, and perhaps a little lye if the paintwork is very dirty, this corrosive solution is applied with brooms and washed off with the hose.

A deckhand wears rubber boots if he doesn't want the skin eaten off his feet. It is rough on the hands, too, but after a time your hands get hardened to it, even if it takes some of the paint off the ship.

When you get through a day's soogeying, the cabins are snow white. Everything gleams . . . except the deckhands.

The *Cravanette* reached the Soo. This time the mate sent me down the ladder onto the lock wall to handle the lines. I enjoyed feeling important while the tourists at the locks watched me struggle, dragging the heavy steel cable to the bollard on the lock wall. When the ship was tied up in the lock, the mate told me to get back aboard if I didn't want to get left. The lock men would throw the lines off when the ship had risen to the Lake Superior level and was ready to go.

The whole operation took but forty-five minutes.

Fifteen hours later, the ship docked at Marquette, Michigan. I was conscious of a lump in my throat as I looked across the harbor at the city of my birth, from which my family had moved to Cleveland some eight years before. I hadn't seen the place since that time, and yet it looked as familiar as if I had left only a week before. I asked Roy about going ashore.

"Ashore!" he exclaimed. "Deckhands stay on deck all the time we are loading. Every time they move the ship, you have to go on the dock to handle the lines. Nobody ever heard of a deckhand going ashore while the boat is at an ore dock."

It was a blow. And throughout the summer, each time we got to Marquette, I felt the old town calling me, but I couldn't answer.

The season was full. I learned to tie the bowline, the square knot, the sheet bend, various hitches. I learned to

Deckhand going over the side in docking operations. (Alan W. Sweigert photo.)

splice using short splice, eye splice, and long splice. I learned to coil a heaving line and throw it accurately.

When fall blew in, it was rugged going. The temperature iced the decks. The sun no longer shone. The seas rose steel gray, and the skies were lead. Autumn storms pierced wool.

Nearing the end of the season, the sailors still called me Slim, but the description hardly fit anymore.

Arriving at Buffalo at the end of a trip, we went forward for our pay—one dollar per day. Captain Buchanan counted it out as we signed the payroll in his office.

Captains and mates don't spend many words telling a deckhand how he did or praising him up. But they talk to each other, from port to port and ship to ship. Captain Buchanan didn't give me any elaborate good-bye as I left the *Charlotte Graveraet Breitung*. But, as it happened, Captain J. L. Bradshaw, who commanded the *E. N. Breitung*, was transferring next season to command of the *Centurion*. He asked me to go with him next summer when school was out.

I guess that was my report card.

When I went home that fall, school seemed tame.

CHAPTER II

FIRE HOLD
UNIVERSITY

I took the train to Buffalo, where the *Centurion* was unloading grain at the pool elevator on the lakefront. Arriving on board, I found there was no opening available in the forward end, and Captain Bradshaw asked me if I didn't want to pass coal for a trip or two until something opened up in the deck department. I didn't relish the fire hold, but I agreed.

The old *Centurion* was fast but antiquated. Her fire hold had side bunkers, which necessitated wheeling the coal into the fire hold with a wheelbarrow to put it in reach of the firemen. Coal dust and ashes covered me from head to foot and penetrated my pores until I soon looked like the Greek fireman on the *C. G. Breitung*. I wasn't happy, but pride made me stick. There wasn't anywhere else I could go on this boat.

I stood watches—six hours on, six off. Sam Bronski, the fireman in my watch, friendly rough and a mountain of a man, showed me the routine: wheel the coal from the bunkers and dump it opposite the firebox doors in piles where Sam could shovel it into the fires.

Once each watch, Sam pulled the fires, with a long steel hoe, dragging white-hot coals right out onto the fire hold deck, while I threw buckets of water on the flaming pile to quench it. The heat was above two hundred degrees. I dared not stand too close, lest I burn my face and clothes. I wore canvas gloves, and Sam told me to wear a wool shirt. I thought the fireman was kidding me, but no—a woolen shirt keeps the heat off you better than anything. I perspired gallons when the fires were pulled down onto the deck, and my face became sunburned. The heat didn't seem to burn the grin off Sam's red, sweat-bright face. He loved the work and took great pride in it.

Next, I was to pull the ashes out from under the grates with the steel hoe, also hot work, though not as killing as pulling the fires.

Sam introduced me to the ash gun, a hopper mounted in the forward side of the fire hold next to the bulkhead. From the bottom of the hopper, a six-inch pipe slanted up so that its mouth went through the wide-plating of the ship, above the waterline. A smaller water connection led into the base from the opposite side.

"When you get ready to shoot the ashes, go back between the boilers into the engine room and tell the oiler to start the pump. Be sure to have the valve open first, or the pressure will bust the waterline. Then you shovel the ashes into the hopper, and the water pressure will shoot 'em up the pipe and overboard."

That wasn't hard, except that it meant a lot more shoveling—and my back already ached from shoveling mountains of coal. I opened the valve as I had been instructed, then went back between the boilers to the engine room and told the oiler to start the pump. When I returned to the fire hold, the water under high pressure was making a hissing roar in the ash gun, but the water went up the pipe and overboard and didn't seem to get out into the hold. So I started shoveling the hill of ashes into the hopper. The instant I threw a shovelful in, it disappeared with a snort and a gurgle up the pipe and overboard, carried by the force of water. I enjoyed it.

Then I lifted a shovelful of ashes with a large, jagged clinker in it. Suddenly a flooding explosion of water hit me in the face and knocked my hat off! I jumped aside and ran to the corner of the fire hold. In two seconds, the torrent of water filled the hopper and poured out onto the floor. Sam yelled, "Tell 'em to shut off the pump—quick!"

I was back in the engine room in a flash, screaming at the oiler, who, grinning broadly, cut off the steam so that the pump ceased pounding. He laughed. "Got a clinker in it, eh?"

I went back to the fire hold, and Sam showed me how to break up clinkers with a bar. I started the pump again and finished shooting the ashes.

Sam advised me that if I worked hard and kept the coal piled up and the ashes cleaned out, I would do all right. I found, after I got accustomed to the constant shoveling, that it became easier. I even had time to sit down occasionally and rest.

I tried firing the boilers, but that was a real job. Throwing a scoopful of coal into the firebox was one thing, but throwing it way back to the farthest part of the firebox and distributing it evenly over the fire, that was something else again. I practiced at it and was improving. But my respect for the fireman increased enormously when I watched and realized the consummate skill with which Sam kept the steam up to one hundred eighty pounds, watching the steam gauge, then throwing in three or four shovels of coal. If the fires got too hot, the safety valve would let go, and that would be from bad firing and a waste of coal.

One day I woke up to find the steamer rolling in a good-sized sea on Lake Michigan. As I went on watch, I had a little trouble descending the ladder to the fire hold. The ladder leaned first one way, then the other. Reaching the bottom safely, however, I watched with fascination as Sam threw open a firebox door and, balancing against the roll of the ship, calmly shoveled coal into the fire. Now and then he missed it as the *Centurion* took a quick lunge, and the coal flew all over the deck.

I had a lot of trouble that watch, filling the wheelbarrow which showed a tendency to tip over and wanting to go any direction but straight. The coal slid around the deck. The worst part of it was that when I threw a shovelful, it didn't land where I intended. The rolling vessel made it a trick to toss the ashes into the ash gun. About every other shovelful missed the hopper and littered the deck. It was one busy watch.

Passing coal was dirty and hot.

I never managed to get my skin clean. And I was so tired that about all I ever did while off watch was sleep. For another thing, down in the fire hold you couldn't see where the ship was going, which is a large part of the pleasure of sailing.

It was a huge relief when the first mate told me on the last day of the two-week trip that I was to take my gear over on the other side of the cabin to the deckhands' room. I washed off coal dust for the last time.

In the language of the lake sailors, the *Centurion* was a *home*.

She was towing the old wooden barge *Chickamauga* that year, and she plodded along on her way, in no haste. There was little work to be done, and Captain Bradshaw pampered the deckhands. He was a gentleman, jovial and thoughtful. Sometimes when we were painting on deck, he would come by on his way forward from breakfast, his pockets bulging with oranges. With a quick look around to make sure the first mate wasn't watching, he would hand us deckhands each an orange. "To hold you until dinner."

The time you appreciate a ship like that is when you get your next ship.

BATTLE OF THE SECTIONS

Came another summer, I shipped out on the *Col. James M. Schoonmaker*. She and her 8,603-gross-ton sister ship, *William P. Snyder, Jr.*, were the largest freighters on the Great Lakes [1918], and we were proud to be part of her crew.

As the gray of predawn changed gradually to the full-flaming miracle of sunrise on Lake Superior, I was reminded of Omar's lines:

> Awake, for morning in the bowl of night has flung the stone that put
> the stars to flight;
> And lo, the hunter of the East has caught the Sultan's turret in a
> noose of light.

The 12,200-ton-capacity freighter quietly made her way dead slow in through the piers at Allouez, the Superior

Colonel James M. Schoonmaker. (Photo courtesy of the Great Lakes Historical Society.)

Str. *William P. Snyder, Jr.* (Alan W. Sweigert photo.)

Loading the bulk carriers was always a straight gravity shot.

entrance to the Duluth Harbor. With faces expressionless, two fishermen sitting on the breakwater watched the great green-sided steamer silently pass. She turned to starboard inside the harbor, and then to port, and finally moored at the ore dock.

It was the first day of July. The deckhands had divided up into two crews and were removing the hatches in competition. She was a thirty-five-hatch boat, and each crew had about eighteen hatches to uncover.

There was a reward for loading the *Schoonmaker* in a hurry, for if she managed to get back to Cleveland on the morning of the Fourth of July [Saturday], the vessel would not commence unloading until Monday, and we would have a two-day holiday, a rare thing. Cleveland deckhands could go home. The men were in high spirits that morning, and the two crews worked with a will at pulling off the

It was the *unloading* that tried men's ingenuity and gave rise to the invention of the darndest monsters.

hatch covers. One deckhand in each crew was handling the bridle and one the steel tripod which carried a sheave in its apex to lead the light steel cable forward or aft to the winch.

I had the tripod. Our crew was leading the race. Wally, the deckhand at the bridle, raced to the next hatch and placed the bridle rings over the buttons on the hatch while I pulled the pin in the shackle and rushed the heavy steel tripod along the deck to the next hatch. Wally raised his arm in a highball signal to the bos'n; the bos'n opened the steam valve on the winch. I didn't quite manage to get the pin into the ring bolt in the deck, and the next instant I was swept across the deck by the cable and brought up

In some ports the vessel had to be moved along the dock several times to match up cargo holds with unloading buckets.

Onboard cranes on deck rails were developed. They could be fitted with buckets or with magnets for unloading scrap. (Photo courtesy of the Dutton Collection.)

Finally the self-unloader with a system of conveyor belts freed some carriers from shoreside unloaders. (Photo courtesy of the Dutton Collection.)

against the corner of a hatch with the steel tripod on top of me. I was knocked unconscious.

I came to a few minutes later, got up, and stumbled forward to my bunk in the fo'c'sle.

In my haste, I had ignored the safety rule against standing inside the bight of the cable. Wally had broken a rule, too—he had given a "heave away" signal without making certain everyone was in the clear. Only the watchfulness of the bos'n at the winch saved my life; he had shut off the steam and reversed the winch the instant he saw me swept across the deck. It was a close thing.

In a few minutes, the first mate came down. Seeing that I was not dead, he ordered, "Back on deck, mister."

Welcome to steamboating, Dutton!

Sections, sections, sections! These were something you could really hate. I cursed and swore at the sections, along with the rest of the crew.

Sections were stagings made from three-inch white oak planks, held together with steel angle irons. Hung by chains from six-inch oak strongbacks laid across the open hatches, they were used to throw the iron ore farther over in the hold as it flowed from the dock spouts, for the big steamship was so broad of beam that the spouts were not long enough to trim the ore to the outer side of the ship and load her on an even keel.

Hour after hour, the crew sweated and swore at the sections, placing one in a hatchway and letting it down to the proper angle, then pulling it up and moving it over a little, and then to the next hatch, skipping around here and there as the need arose, and thus loading the vessels, with back-breaking work. One of the sections hung in each of the thirty-five hatches, and they used them in all. After six hours of this labor, the crew was exhausted.

Whenever sailors who worked these wide ships gathered in a tavern, the sections were consigned to hell.

Eventually someone thought to lengthen the dock spouts a few feet, and sections became history, unmourned.

The *Schoonmaker* loaded and sailed. She docked at Cleveland Saturday morning. I got two days at home.

I used a lot of it to bellyache about the horrors of the fire hold and the sections. It would be many years before I learned that the fire hold and the sections were the school for battalions of young men who used that tough training to condition themselves for the rugged climb up the executive ladders of America's corporations.

CHAPTER III

ABLE SEAMAN . . .
THE HARD WAY

Assuming a swagger I didn't feel, I climbed the stairs to Cleveland's shipping hall on West Ninth Street on an April afternoon in the 1920s. I strode up to the counter and hit old Prince for a berth.

He glanced at my brand new A.B. certificate.

"A.B., are you?" barked Prince.

I deepened my voice a little, as I'd seen many an able seaman do. "Yes, sir!"

"I'll send you to Lorain. They need a wheelsman on the *Superior City.*" He wrote out a slip and handed it to me. Then he called to another chap sitting at a desk behind the counter. "Jim, take this guy over and buy him a ticket to Lorain."

The reason for this was that there was always the chance a sailor might be diverted and fritter away the ticket money on some strong waters shoreside, forgetting the ship. Other times a sailor might have no intention of shipping out. Sailors were scarce that year, and when one showed up, the

GREAT LAKES LOADING PORTS

POTASH
Thunder Bay

MINNESOTA

LIMESTONE
Port Inland
Cedarville
Drummond Island
Calcite
Stoneport
Marblehead

GYPSUM
Port Gypsum
Alabaster

GRAIN
Thunder Bay
Duluth
Superior
Milwaukee
Chicago
Saginaw
Sarnia
Toledo
Huron

IRON ORE
Duluth
Superior
Two Harbors
Taconite Harbor
Marquette
Escanaba

COAL
Superior
Thunder Bay
Chicago
Toledo
Sandusky
Ashtabula
Conneaut

CEMENT
Charlevoix
Alpena
Bath

PETROLEUM
East Chicago
Sarnia
Toledo

Map courtesy of the Lake Carriers' Association.

Lake Carriers' Association wanted to be sure he got to the boat.

When the Lake Shore interurban pulled into Lorain, I was met as I stepped off the car by a shipping hall runner who drove me to the shipyard where the 7,800-ton freighter *General Orlando M. Poe* was lying. The runner explained that the *Superior City* on which I was ticketed was not ready to sail, whereas the *Poe* was ready but for one A.B.

After sending my suitcase up the ship's side on a heaving line tossed down by a sailor, I climbed the ladder to the deck. No sooner was I aboard than the mooring lines were cast off. The steamer proceeded downriver behind a tug. The first mate greeted me, showed me my room and berth in the Texas, and asked, "Can you steer?"

"A little," I replied, secure in the knowledge that the ship was already outside the piers.

"Well, I'll be a damned. The landlubbers they send us for sailors—can't steer, can't splice, can't even tie a bowline!" The mate swore in blue italic several minutes. "By God, you'll learn to steer, or else go over the side before the trip is finished!"

The very first time on watch, the mate told me to take the wheel. The big 470-foot light freighter was slamming along into a little chop on the course from the Middle Ground to Bar Point, at the mouth of the Detroit River.

GREAT LAKES RECEIVING PORTS

Map courtesy of the Lake Carriers' Association.

47

The weather was clear and cold. So I took the wheel, grasping the spokes and spreading my feet a little in the manner I'd seen it done so often before. But a surge of helpless fright came over me. It didn't seem possible that I could control that great steamship and hold her in her course. When I had watched another wheelsman do it, it had always seemed easy.

Well, in a minute the vessel began to sheer off course, according to the turning of the lubber mark on the compass card. So I turned the wheel a spoke or two. Let's see, I thought. I have to turn the wheel in the opposite direction from the way I want to go. Vessels steered by crossed chains in those days, and it added a little spice to operations to have to turn the wheel the wrong way. But nothing happened. The freighter kept right on turning—a point, two points. So, a little more scared, I gave her some more wheel, wondering as I did if I wasn't turning the wheel the wrong way after all. Finally, she stopped swinging and started back the other way. When she got back on her course, I put the wheel amidships, beginning to feel a bit proud of myself. But I received a rude shock. That steamer kept right on swinging to port! Remembering the crossed chains again, I put the wheel over two or three spokes to port; still she continued her swing. Then I turned the wheel a whole turn, by this time in full panic. She stopped and slowly started back again.

Good grief, I thought. How do you ever keep this wagon on course?

All this time, the first mate was standing off to one side, grinning. "Well, at least you *said* you couldn't steer much, and by the great horn spoon I believe you!"

Finally he relented. Pushing me to one side, he took the wheel and quickly and skillfully steadied her up on her course.

"Meet 'er, do you see?" he said. "Meet 'er, before she

starts to move. Anticipate what she's going to do before she does it, and never use too much wheel. Just a spoke or two, like this." And he gave the big wheel a couple of spokes to starboard. He turned the wheel back to me, and I tried again. After a time, I began to get a little of the feel of it, managing to keep the steamer somewhere within a point or two of her course, though the ship showed a perverse tendency to stray off to one side or the other, like a horse with a green rider.

We were approaching Bar Point Light now, the watch was changed, and with immeasurable relief I went below to stand the lookout for two hours. Six hours on and six off was the rule. The lake vessels were carrying six A.B.s that year, and a man stood two hours at the wheel, two hours on the lookout, and two on deck. No watchmen or deck watches were carried.

Through several watches—during which I was not permitted to steer the freighter in the rivers at all—I gradually caught on and began to get the hang of it. By the time the ship was nearing Duluth, I was feeling pretty cocky again. Whistling and talking with the mate and the skipper, I was managing to hold her fairly well within a half point of her course.

The mate said nothing, just smiled.

Duluth—and the *Poe* was loading 9,000 tons of iron ore. It was enjoyable to run the winches, moving the ship along the dock from time to time, spotting her hatches under different sets of ore spouts. She was finally loaded, the wooden hatch covers were in place, and the tarpaulins battened down for the trip back downlakes to Lorain.

It was nighttime when I went on watch again. The mate seemed to enjoy standing to my port beam and grinning.

But I confidently took the wheel, and when the vessel swung a bit from her course, I gave her a couple of spokes to bring her back. But there was something wrong! She kept

Several groups in several ports are endeavoring to restore some of these surviving great ladies of the once grand passenger trade (photos pp. 50–52). (W. A. McDonald photos.)

on swinging. I tried some more wheel, and then some more, and she reluctantly stopped sheering off and came back again, only to yaw far over to the other side—three whole points before I could stop her! I felt cold all over and yelled to the mate, "There's something wrong, sir. I can't make her settle down!"

The mate unlipped a humorless laugh. "Of course she steers much harder loaded than light. Takes a little more wheel to stop her, and be damn careful not to let her get away from you."

I concentrated.

"You ought to steer one of these crates when it is loaded down some by the head," he volunteered. "Then you'd need to know something."

Two or three watches later, by the time the steamer had passed Whitefish Point and was nearing the Soo River the following day, I was again feeling pretty good and had convinced myself that I was a wheelsman. I had mastered the big steamer! The old girl was eating out of my hand! Point Iroquois was abeam when I took the wheel, and the ship was heading on the Birch Point Range. Captain Mallory perched on his stool looking out the front window, conning the ship. I began to get a little jumpy, expecting that any moment the skipper would have another man to relieve me, for the ship was getting down into the St. Marys River. The channel was narrowing; other ships passed upbound from time to time, pretty close aboard. Captain Mallory straightened up but never said a word about it. Soon he gave the order, "Starboard some."

He looked at me as I cautiously put the wheel over a half a turn, which looked like a whole lot to me. Slowly the big steamer started to turn to port.

"Faster." The skipper spoke sharply.

I gave her a full turn this time.

"A little more," he ordered. "Let her come around now, let her come around."

Casting discretion aside, I gave her another turn of starboard helm, and it looked as though the ship would turn right around. Her stern was swinging madly, and I was resigned to expecting the very worst.

Finally, the skipper called out, "Slow," whereupon I began spinning the wheel madly back to port—three full turns to the other side, around and around and around. Maybe I could stop her after all!

"Look out!" said the skipper. "Don't stop her. Let her come now; let her come slow."

I put the wheel amidships. The steamer slowly continued her turning.

The next order was "Steady her there," and I put the wheel a good full turn to port again. The ship stopped swinging and started back to starboard.

"Watch out!" barked the skipper. "Steady her—steady her!"

I finally managed to get the Poe steadied on the new course, lining up her steering pole on the new range lights ahead. My heart ceased pounding, and a feeling of confidence gradually oozed back into my bones.

Looking ahead, with a shock I saw a huge ore carrier bearing down on us—almost dead ahead! Sweat began to pour from my face. I turned the wheel to port a little to edge over out of the other ship's way.

"Easy now," the captain ordered. "Don't run her ashore. Keep her in the channel." Gingerly, I edged the wheel to starboard, all the while watching the approaching steamer with apprehension.

"Port a little," he called then. "Bring her over a little more."

I was completely up in the air by this time. Rattled, I put the big wheel the wrong way.

Instantly, the captain pushed me away from the wheel. With a couple of quick turns back and forth, he settled the steamer down on her course once more. We passed the other steamer with a hundred feet to spare.

My legs shaking, I waited for the skipper to relieve me, wishing I were miles away, anyplace but in that damned pilothouse.

But Captain Mallory said, "All right, son, you can take her."

My knees were oatmeal, and I felt nothing but empty inside; but I took the wheel again.

I was surprised to find I had no trouble bringing the ship around past Pte. Aux Pins and heading her down for the locks. I even steered her down into the lock until she was tied up to the wall.

When I went below to man the winches, I was whistling. My partner took over as the steamer moved out of the lock. Off watch, I stood on deck with the careless posture of experience, watching the few people on the lock wall.

I had no trouble that amounted to much the rest of the trip down Lake Huron and through the St. Clair and Detroit rivers, and when the big steamer pulled into Lorain two days later, the first mate called me and paid me off. I was somewhat regretful; I liked the vessel and crew. With a shrug, I went about packing up. My heart was light as I made my way through the steel mill yards, casually dodging trains of ore and slag cars pushed by busy switch engines.

The next morning, I was at the shipping office again, grinning confidently. I was a wheelsman, make no mistake about it!

CHAPTER IV

THE SEA VS. DUTTON

Since I now knew all there was to know, it should be smooth sailing.

My next vessel was the 7,800-ton-capacity *J. F. Durston.* She was a *home* in sailor language—a ship for a sailor to stick to all season long—comfortable quarters, good mates, good food, not too much work. And a competent skipper, Captain Det Parsons, out of Vermilion, Ohio.

After a few bad moments steering in the rivers on the first trip, I soon settled into the life of the ship, finding it easy to steer in the narrowest channels. Running the many ranges in the rivers soon became no trick, and I quickly learned to stand at the wheel facing the after end of the ship and holding her smokestack in line with the ranges—a procedure that is a bit difficult to master. It necessitates turning the wheel the opposite way each time to make her stern swing in the right direction. It was a new kind of steering that had to be learned all over again.

I learned to keep my eye on the stern when taking her through the locks at the Soo. I learned to let her stern

J. F. Durston. (Photo courtesy of the Dutton Collection.)

swing ever so gently up against the wall with only the slightest bump. I learned to steer the ship at a snail's pace along the walls above and below the locks, always keeping her stern a few feet off, so that I would let neither her bow nor her stern swing out. This is appreciated by the deckhands holding the steel mooring cables; it prevents yanking them into the canal.

And I learned to steer a straight course in the open lake, keeping the ship's head within an eighth of a point. I even amused myself on occasion steering by watching the shadow of the window frame on the floor. But this meant adjusting the reference point every five minutes or so on account of the movement of the sun.

The last trip of the year that fall, I shipped out on the *Willis L. King*, a big 580-foot freighter, for a run up to Manitowoc on Lake Michigan with a load of coal, and then light to Allouez [Superior] for iron ore.

It was pretty cold on Lake Superior that last half of November, and part of my duty was sounding the ballast tanks. While it was fairly hard work, I thought it would be routine. I went along the deck and dropped a sounding rod on a length of light line into the wells in each tank. These were pipes that led into the deck, reaching clear to the bottom of the ship. There were fourteen of these wells—six on either side of the deck, one in the forepeak, and one in the afterpeak. Accordingly, at the end of each watch I had to arm myself with sounding rod, line, a small blackboard, a piece of carpenter's chalk, a rag for wiping off the rod, and, in the night watch, a lantern. Bundled up in sweaters and oilskins, rubber boots, and a sou'wester hat, I'd proceed along the deck, stopping at each sounding well and dropping the rod into the pipe, letting the line run out until the rod touched bottom, thirty-two feet below. Then, pulling up the line, I would quickly read the depth of water shown

Str. *Willis L. King*. (Photo courtesy of the Great Lakes Historical Society.)

on the rod, wipe off the rod, mark the reading on the blackboard, and proceed to the next well.

That worked fine in summer, but this was on Superior in fall.

In freezing weather, ice formed on the rod. I had to melt off the ice with bare hands. I was always glad to finish the job and get back aft to the warm engine room to copy the soundings on the pilothouse blackboard.

Then, on one watch a northwest gale screamed into the rigging as the ship wallowed along up Lake Superior toward Manitou Island Light. Huge soot-colored seas reared out of the opaque gloom, tearing at the ship's fo'c'sle, often rising far above the bulwarks and smashing against the observation cabin and even the pilothouse windows. Ripping aft along the vessel's sides, the great seas flooded the deck from rail to rail.

Watching my chance, I ran from under the shelter of the fo'c'sle house. Sliding across the film of ice on the deck, I brought up at the sounding well to number one port tank, quickly flipping the well cap open and dropping the sounding rod into the well. Above the gale, I heard the hissing, crashing roar of a sea boarding the ship from the starboard. Dropping the line, I dove back to the fo'c'sle, grabbing the companionway railing in time to save myself, holding on until the sea passed and spent itself over the side.

With a wary eye to windward, I tried again. Grasping the end of the line in the well, I began pulling up the rod. Frantically heaving on the line, I got the rod clear of the well as another great comber loomed over the starboard rail. But I slipped on the deck ice and flung out my hands to grab the wire rail as the sea caught me and swept me toward the ship's side. I hung on. When the torrent receded, it left me hanging on to the rail, half drowned.

I didn't stop to look for the rod and the other sounding equipment, most of which had gone over the side. I'd almost reached the companionway leading up to the fo'c'sle deck when the next sea overtook me, and again I was picked up and carried along; but this time the wave threw me into the corner of the port fo'c'sle wing. Struggling up again, I got safely into the hallway and slammed the door before the next sea came.

A routine chore at sea can become a news event if Mother Nature decides to laugh at you.

It was cold on the lakes in November, often around zero, icing the decks. The watch on the lookout wasn't bad while in the open lake, for then the lookout was permitted to stand his watch in the wheelhouse, keeping a sharp eye peeled for other vessels, lights, and dangers. But in the rivers, you stand lookout watch out there on the fo'c'sle head—rain, cold, or snow.

Sometimes it was impossible to make one's way back to the after cabin for the seas sweeping the deck; and on occasion the forward crew went hungry twenty-four hours or more. There was a lifeline rigged from the forward cabin to the boiler-house aft—a steel cable with lines hanging down, so that a sailor could hang on when a sea came aboard. But if the seas were really big, it was a brave man or a damned fool who would attempt that walk.

Coffee was all we had on such occasions. The watchman was charged with serving coffee at midnight, or at two A.M., in the pilothouse. But coffee is more than coffee. In my watch on the *King*, the watchman appeared at midnight with the percolator, cups, sugar, and the cow—condensed milk. He poured coffee for me, the second mate, and himself, then relieved me at the wheel for half an hour. It was then that the talk was at its best—of ships and shore adventures and wild escapades. Here we settled the affairs of the company, the nation, and the human race. The night watches were always best.

MAJOR MARINE HAZARD

Perhaps the worst hazard involved on the lake freighter for both crew and officers is food. There is no discrimination in this regard; all are served the same.

A lot has been written about the deep-water hell ships, with starvation vittles, salt horse, and hardtack crawling with weevils. The trouble on these lake freighters is the reverse. The food is too good, too rich, too plentiful— ham, pork sausages, roast beef, roast pork, steaks, chops, chicken, duck, turkey, together with cakes, pies, and other gourmet delights.

Looking around at the young sailors already going to suet at thirty and some mates of only forty waddling like sea lions, I knew I had to protect myself. I was aware I was no longer called Slim.

It was always a troublesome problem for me, and I got around it by skipping at least one meal each day. This was brutal hardship, for the food was so fragrant. There was a terrible temptation to put off the omitted meal until the next time. Even on two meals a day, I found it hard to avoid being half sick a large part of the time, simply from overeating.

The firemen and coal passers need this heavy food; they burn up a lot of energy shoveling coal and ashes, pulling fires, and hauling clinkers. But catfish will speak Chinese before the rest of the crew will burn off half the food they eat.

Here is Thanksgiving dinner on the *Poe*: fruit cocktail, oyster cocktail, crab cocktail with cocktail sauce, stuffed celery, olives ripe and stuffed, cream of mushroom soup, chef's salad, roast turkey with chestnut dressing, roast Long Island duck with apple dressing, Virginia ham, fried chicken, giblet gravy, cranberry sauce, asparagus tips, baked Hubbard squash, duchess potatoes, candied sweet potatoes, Parkerhouse rolls, pumpkin pie, mince pie, apple pie, plum pudding with brandy sauce, mint ice, Neapolitan ice cream, light and dark fruitcake, assorted cookies, candies and nuts, figs and dates, coffee, tea, milk, cider, Catawba wine, bourbon, scotch, beer, cigars, cigarettes . . . and toothpicks.

You can't eat it all, but you can hardly resist it. So shrewd professionals choose what they can handle (and a bit more) and let the rest go. Pretty near all the crew (except the youthful deckhands who haven't learned their lesson) do the same. And what happens to the rest that's left over? Over the side for the gulls. With no hard feelings to the gulls, it was a terrible waste.

The steamship companies have tried to do something about it. The marine superintendent has tried instructing the stewards to serve smaller portions. But then the crew starts bitching about the company being a "poor feeder." So they serve everything but the ship's geraniums and throw away leftovers.

Passing down at Detour one afternoon, there was a man in a skiff resting on his oars ahead of us. The skipper checked down to bare steerageway as the man came alongside. The steward let down a pail on a light line, and the man put into it four beautiful Lake Superior whitefish, receiving forty cents in return. The entire crew had whitefish for supper. I wonder what it would cost today.

OFF WATCH

There's not a great deal of truth in the saying that sailors are a carefree lot. On the Great Lakes, few, if any, sailors have a girl in every port. The ship pulls into Duluth or Allouez or Two Harbors or Marquette. Two minutes after the lines are on the dock, the ore spouts are down, and the red stuff is flowing into the cargo hold. In less than an hour, the ship is moved along the dock a ship-length or two, and the second run is put in, shortly followed by the third run, and the fourth if required. A few more cars of ore are loaded to trim the ship, and she's gone. They take from two to six hours to load a freighter; the average is about three and a half.

The poor devil of a sailor is afraid to stay ashore more than a couple of hours for fear his ship will sail without him. The skipper won't hold her there even five minutes. When she's loaded, the lines are cast off, and she sails. The sailor has time for maybe a beer or two, and maybe he gets to buy a few postcards and a paper; he seldom finds time for a haircut. A lot of times he doesn't even get a chance to get off the ship; he buys what he needs from the bumboat which usually ties up alongside for an hour while the ship is at the dock.

Three or four days later, he's ashore again, if he's off watch, at Cleveland or Lorain or Conneaut, or Buffalo perhaps. And it takes from four to six hours to unload the cargo. Seldom does he find time for looking up a girlfriend. Same old story, couple of beers.

The sailor off watch reads books and magazines and writes letters. One of the principal diversions is poker in the dunnage room. The skipper discourages card games, which often lead to bad feelings and fights. But the dunnage room is outside the skipper's bailiwick; he never goes down below, and what he doesn't know won't hurt him. So sometimes you'll see a sailor lose his entire pay in one poker sitting.

The *John A. McGean*. (Photo courtesy of the Great Lakes Historical Society.)

The mates and engineers often join in the game, for they are lesser human beings, too; but not the captain. The skipper must not descend. He must stay up there on the pedestal where he belongs if he expects crew performance.

Usually someone is found among the crew who is an amateur barber. Often he serves as barber to the entire crew, including the captain. The captain and mates have even less time ashore than the rest of the crew, so without an onboard barber they would be really hairy.

I was at the wheel one Sunday afternoon on the old 8,000-ton freighter *George Simonson*. The captain was a good man but a stickler on two things: trim hair on sailors and proper respect for ship's officers. One of the vain, long-haired deckhands stuck his head in the door, and although he saw the captain standing there, he entered and sat down in the captain's high chair. There was a hung silence awaiting the captain's reaction. The skipper got out the barber tools and, to the amusement of the watchers, proceeded to cut the deckhand's hair, real close. "Now you not only sit like a captain, sonny, you look like a captain."

CHAPTER V

"NOTHING
TO THE LEFT!"

The Wheelsman's Axiom is "Meet her and anticipate what she is going to do before she does it."
But how can you . . . ?

When you take a steamer light, up through the forty
miles of the St. Marys River on a fine, bright summer
afternoon, running the ranges, holding the steering pole
right on the mark ahead, turning at the proper moment
coming abreast of one of the quick-flash buoys, and finally
come around out of the Little Rapids Cut and head her on
the land spit between the locks and the St. Marys Falls, and
then you swing her a little more and lay her bow alongside
the pier below the lock with hardly a bump—*that's a fine
thing*!

You are really living the life of the gods.

Then you let the big steamer slide along the wall and into
the lock until she is tied up and the gates close behind her.

That is living.

The skipper goes ashore to the lock office for dispatches and the mail, and you go down on deck and buy a newspaper from the boy with the cart alongside on the lock wall. You watch a little fascinated as, with the ship rising in the lock, the boy makes change and dexterously tosses the merchandise, together with the change, up to the sailors on deck ten or fifteen feet over his head.

"Catch it on the way *up*," he calls. That way, money seldom falls into the lock.

And nothing you read in the newspaper you buy comes anywhere near close to steamboating.

You handle the winches until the lock is filled and the ship is ready to cast off again—no more than twenty minutes or half an hour later. Then you dash back up to the wheelhouse to take her out. The skipper rings full ahead on the Chadburn, and she starts to move. You don't have much room on either side to let her swing. You have to be darn careful not to let her bump either wall!

"SHE'LL HIT THE WALL, CAPTAIN"

I was bringing the 9,000-ton *Gamaliel Johnston* into the MacArthur Lock upbound on a dark night, and it was necessary to tie up below the lock to let a downbound vessel through. When that ship cleared, our captain ordered the lines let go and rang slow ahead, at the same time ordering me "right a little" to keep her stern off the wall. There is a bend in the wall just below the lock which makes it awkward to bring a steamer around and into the lock. Always, in moving along the wall to enter the lock, it is necessary to keep the ship's bow against the wall and her stern a few feet off; otherwise, her bow would swing out from the wall, and you lose control. And you have to remember always that when you back the engines, a vessel's stern will swing left and her bow to the right.

As the *Johnston* crept slowly around the bulge in the wall, I kept her stern a dozen feet off, but when she got around the bend, the current from the lock caught her, and her forward end moved out into the channel. And thus she moved into the lock—just about in the middle between the piers.

"Left!" ordered the captain, and so I put the wheel left and turned to watch her stern swing slowly toward the right-hand wall, and then put the wheel right to meet her.

"Left some more!" said the captain.

"She'll hit the wall, captain," I reminded him in a quiet voice.

"I don't care; put her left!"

With no further comment, I put the wheel left once more and saw the third mate back aft by the deckhouse frantically waving his arms in an up-and-down scissorslike gesture, meaning there was no more room; her stern would strike the wall.

A grinding thump—the 400-foot freighter struck and bounded off, shaking throughout her length like a dog after a bath. Her bow swung to the right. She seemed determined to do the opposite of what the skipper wanted. She went alongside the right-hand wall, and when the captain rang for full astern to stop her headway, she swung her stern across the lock, and the third mate finally got a stern line across the lock and on a bollard. They ran a heaving line forward along the deck to get the forward lines out and dragged the steamer bodily across the lock with the winches. The mates eventually got her tied up to the left-hand wall, and the lower lock gates closed behind her.

When the gates yawned open ahead, the captain ordered "left," and I gave her a bit of left wheel but checked the swing as her stern neared the wall, and I laid her stern up against the concrete wall without a tremor, and then gave her the left wheel to hold her there. Turning with 2,500 horsepower behind it, the propeller was throwing water against the rudder, making it very easy to swing the ship one way or the other, or to stop her swing exactly where you wanted her.

WHEN AMIDSHIPS IS NOT AMIDSHIPS, THE HEART JUMPS INTO THE MOUTH

The twenty-five-mile run down the St. Marys River from the locks to Mud Lake is the most trying part of the entire trip, at night. With the shallow water—*only a few inches between the bottom of the vessel and the river bottom*—and the three-mile current, it is a treacherous run. Many a vessel has gone on the rocks along this channel.

The deeply laden steamer wants to go anywhere but where she should. Much of the channel is no more than three hundred feet wide, and to let her stray from her course may mean a very cozy grounding on rocky bottom.

Sometimes when a ship goes aground, she may swing across the channel, blocking it completely, and it may not be possible for a steamer following to stop in time to avoid a collision. Government regulations provide that a following vessel shall keep at least a quarter-mile astern of another in the narrower channels. We saw the *Upson* with her bow tucked neatly up in the corner just above the West Neebish rock cut, but her bow was four feet out of water.

Running in shallow water, a loaded ship simply will not go straight ahead with her wheel amidships; instead, she carries a certain amount of right or left rudder. It may be a spoke or two, or it may be as much as one or two whole turns of the steering wheel. I found on one trip that the *Schoonmaker* [on which Dutton had been a deckhand years earlier—Ed.] carried twenty degrees of left rudder in these shallow channels—almost three whole turns of the wheel—which meant that her rudder had to be kept in a position halfway to hard over left in order to keep her straight in the channel.

But this would be all right if you could count on the ship carrying the same amount of rudder one way or the other constantly in shallow water. The worst—the most confusing—problem of the wheelsman is the annoying way that a vessel has of "changing her wheel" without warning. You can get accustomed to steering the ship by mentally shifting the midships position of the wheel a turn or two to one side or the other like transposing a tune into a different key on the piano; but when you have reached the new mental adjustment and begin to devote your attention to keeping the ship on the ranges or the leading light ahead, only to have her change over so that she carries a couple of turns of wheel the other way all of a sudden, it will throw you for a loss every time!

You enter one of these channels, and you "feel her out" gingerly to locate the point where she carries her wheel, and you are beginning to breathe easily in the knowledge that you know where to put the wheel for amidships. And then your heart jumps into your mouth, for she suddenly takes a sheer way off to the left or the right, and in about two seconds it dawns on you that instead of having the wheel amidships, you have it about three or four turns over the other way—you really haven't the slightest idea how far!

And then you frantically claw the spokes over to meet

her swing, without the slightest notion how far you have to turn the wheel to give her enough to meet her. You don't dare give her too much wheel to either side—she'll get away from you, and then you are lost—lost completely. And brother, you don't have any time to go back and start all over again. Those rocks are right over there only about fifty or at most a hundred feet to one side or the other, and that's nothing when you are trying to slam a 600- or 700-foot steamship loaded with 10,000 to 20,000 tons of iron ore down along that channel!

Well, you try two turns of the wheel, just for a wild guess, hoping you are somewhere near right. And you wait to see if she'll stop swinging over toward that buoy.

"Nothing to the left!" the mate warns you in a sharp growl.

"Nothing to the left, sir," you reply, hoping he'll remember the time when he was a wheelsman sweating blood as you are doing at this instant.

Not enough; you try another turn. She's near hard over now! Still not enough. Well, to hell with it, you think to yourself. You slam her hard over, desperate now, knowing full well you'll hardly have time to spin her a full twelve turns to hard over the other way, so as to stop her when she starts to swing back.

Ah-h-h, she slows. She stops swinging. You lean into her now and spin that bloody wheel like a madman. Around and around and around. Ping goes the little bell; she's hard over again. Slam her back again, quick now! Where was it that you thought she'd changed her wheel to this time?

The Wheelsman's Axiom is "Meet her and anticipate what she is going to do before she does it." But how can you meet her if you don't know where she is carrying her wheel? I've asked several skippers about this idiosyncrasy of steamships. They shrug.

It would appear to be the little matter of suction. Where a ship is running a narrow channel in shallow water, she creates a suction from either side. The propeller sucks the water out from under the keel, and it has to flow in from somewhere, so it flows in from each side, all along the ship. And when you are on one side of the channel (as you usually are to let other ships have room), the suction pulls the ship toward the bank. In the rock cuts, you can see her pull the water level down three or four feet on the dikes abreast of you. This suction sometimes causes two vessels to come together, or it may pull you right into the bank.

The wheelsman must take this into account while he is steering. You are approaching another steamer, and he is going to pass you fairly close aboard—say a hundred feet off. Both ships are going full speed; you are passing each other at about twenty-five miles an hour. As his bow gets nearly abreast of your bow, you will automatically put your wheel over a little to the right to equalize this suction. That sounds simple enough, doesn't it?

But the other ship will be astern of you in about thirty seconds. That means that in fifteen seconds, he will be right abreast of you, and the suction on your bow will be neutralized and distributed along the entire length of your ship, pulling you broadside toward the other vessel. And inside another ten or fifteen seconds, his stern will be pulling your stern, and your bow will be heading in the other direction. So what you have to do—all in about thirty seconds—is compensate for a strong pull to the left on your bow, then a sidewise pull on your entire ship, and finally a pull on your stern.

You put your wheel to the right when the other ship's bow is abreast of you. Then you steady her amidships— wherever that is—when he is abreast of your entire length and the suction is balanced; then your stern swings toward

The *Edward N. Breitung.*

him, and you must put your wheel to the left. But not too much—the suction only lasts for a moment.

As soon as you first put your wheel right, you know that almost immediately the swing of the steamer you set in motion will be reinforced by the other ship's pull on your stern. It's the timing of the thing.

And, of course, you hope the wheelsman on the other ship knows this, too.

CHAPTER VI

REFLECTIONS IN THE PILOTHOUSE

KNOWING THE CODE

I knew the iron rule of the lakes: the wheelsman always stands when in the rivers. But I had a problem I knew would show up later.

It would not show while the tugs worked. The tug at the *W. H. McGean's* bow hunkered down as it dragged the big ship up the stream. The ore dock at Conneaut, fastest in the world, had taken only two hours and a half to unload the 11,000 tons of iron ore we brought down from Duluth.

I was idle at the wheel, for with a tug at bow and stern there was no need for steering. The full legal responsibility lay with the two tugs; the freighter was no more than a barge now.

The skipper made a startling outcry as a choking cloud of acrid black smoke from the tug poured around and into the pilothouse, momentarily blinding the captain and me. One

Huletts unloading the Str. *Royalton*. (Alan W. Sweigert photo.)

short blast from the bow tug's whistle—an order to the stern tug to cease pushing—and the bow tug slacked off on the towline while its crew hustled the heavy manila cable around to the forward bitts. There was a sudden chorus of blasts from the tug's exhaust as the tiny vessel strained the towline and nosed the steamer into the corner of the turning basin. Two whistles squeaked in the tug's engine room, and a furious churning of water stopped the steamer's headway, and she was permitted to nudge the concrete pier ever so gently with her stem post. The tug's exhaust took up the unearthly chorus and turned the 479-foot vessel in the turning basin. They headed the ship downstream and backed her into the coal dock slip.

"All right, Fred," the skipper said. "You can go down to your winches now." I left the wheel amidships and went below, taking over the running of the two powerful forward steam winches that moored the vessel.

With the ship spotted in position, the coal dock lowered the spout over our coal bunker. The dock lifted a coal car bodily and turned it over like a box of cereal. The coal spilled out of the car, and in exactly one minute it was lowered, empty. Its place was taken by another. Six cars of coal filled the ship's bunker.

A blast of the steamer's whistle to cast off—I ran up the

Supporting the bulk carriers Dutton sailed was a fleet of work boats—tugs, dredges, ice breakers, bum boats, mail boats, and ship chandler's boats. The chandler's boats rushed replacement parts out to the bulk carriers, which kept on moving while being serviced. (Photo courtesy of the Dutton Collection.)

companionway with difficulty and took the wheel. I had previously banged my knee against a winch cylinder, and the knee was giving me trouble.

The captain rang for half speed ahead. The vessel gathered headway down the channel. With a slight turn to the left while the engines were rung up to full ahead, I took the big ship out between the piers into the open lake. I always enjoyed taking a steamer out of a harbor like that. With the throb of the engines at full speed and the breeze starting to hum in the rigging and pour in the windows, your spirits rose; you were free of the land once more. You could always feel the ship's eagerness to be gone from the harbor's grasp.

Outside the piers, the mate came up to the wheelhouse, taking over. The captain made some comment about the weather and went below. The mate set the course—262 degrees on the gyro, so I put the wheel down a turn, steadying the ship on the course when she came around. I dragged over the high stool and settled down for the afternoon watch. It was good to get my weight off the knee.

That night, when I went on watch again, the steamer was passing Bar Point Light and heading up for the Detroit River. Darkness had settled over the water, and the course ahead was marked on either side by a long line of buoys, red or white to starboard and green or white to port, blinking on and off, as I kept the steamer somewhat to the right side of the channel to give downbound vessels room.

My knee was now giving me sharp pain. After I had stood at the wheel for half an hour, the pain became a real agony,

The wheelsman's view of the turning buoy for exit via the Duluth Ship Canal and the famous landmark, the Ariel Bridge. (Alan W. Sweigert photo.)

and I wondered if I would be able to finish the watch. But pride kept me there. Mates get very bored very quick hearing about a seaman's aches and pains.

It is a custom with the force of law that a wheelsman always stands up while steering a ship in the rivers. This is necessary, for he must be braced to put the wheel over one way or the other to negotiate the many turns in the rivers, and he must be able to steer close on the mark and follow the channels accurately. And your mind is less apt to wander from the business at hand if you stay on your feet.

But by this time I could hardly stand. I didn't want to

risk appearing weak. The skipper was looking ahead, leaning on his elbows on the forward windowsill. The third mate was standing over to the port side of the wheelhouse, watching the ship's course up the Detroit River. It was pitch dark outside, and the only light in the wheelhouse was the dim glow from the inside of the gyro compass repeater.

I'll try it this once, I thought to myself as I surreptitiously pulled the wheelsman's stool over. It was a vast relief to sit down and get my weight off that throbbing knee. I wheeled the freighter on her course up past Ballard's Reef and the Limekiln Crossing.

After a time, I noticed out of the corner of my eye that the third mate was looking at me with a quizzical expression. However, he made no comment. I felt uncomfortable about it, but as the mate said nothing, I remained sitting down. Let him say something if he wants!

The watch slipped away, Detroit was left astern, then Belle Isle, and as I brought the steamer around on Peach Island Range and into Lake St. Clair, the skipper went below, leaving the third mate in charge. No sooner had the captain closed the pilothouse door than the mate exploded. "Well, I'll be a doubled-dyed S.O.B.! I've sailed these lakes fifteen years, and that's the first time I ever saw a blasted wheelsman sitting on his stool in the rivers!"

My ears burning, I explained in some embarrassment that I had hit my knee against the winch and it was bothering me considerably, and I thought perhaps the third mate wouldn't mind just this once, under the circumstances.

The third mate surprised me. He came as close to apologizing as a mate can. He asked me to come down to the mate's room when the watch ended and get some liniment for the knee.

The ship passed along through the night.

KNOWING WHERE YOU ARE IS EVERYTHING

One of the worst sensations in the pilothouse is not know-ing exactly where you are.

One night in Lake Superior, I was standing outside on the bridge. Alone up there in the black void, I felt near to finding the answer to the great mystery of life itself. It was one of those rare moments when I felt far from all earthly things. Where are we really, in relation to those other stars?

Suddenly I came to with a start, realizing that I was due on watch. On the lakes, you better know exactly where you are. As I turned to the pilothouse door, I thought of the line from an old poem: "How I pity those poor folks on land!"

Devil's Island light was flashing alternate red and white on the starboard quarter. I watched it for a minute or two, thinking of that dark, remote, mysterious island of basalt and granite and red sandstone, with its mantle of ever-greens. The Apostle Islands—a strange name, that; there were considerably more than twelve of them in the group, and not one of them named for any of the apostles: Devil's Island, Madeleine Island, Outer Island, Michigan Island, and so on.

I opened the wheelhouse door, greeting the other watch. "Good evening, sailors." Then, taking the wheel and repeat-ing the course given me by the wheelsman on watch, I perched myself up on the stool and settled down for the four-hour trick.

Reaching over across the wheel, I adjusted the gyro com-pass repeater and the magnifying glass which brought the other rim of the compass card into better focus. Casting my gaze abeam, I again noted the blinking eye that was Devil's Island light and remarked to the third mate, "From the

Early *Morgan* class pilothouse, with wheel, stand, magnetic compass, and telegraph. Later vessels have bow thruster controls and electric telegraphs, which were installed in the early 1950s. (Alan W. Sweigert photo.)

tables in Bowditch, I figure we ought to be able to see the light for twenty-two miles."

Laughing scornfully, the third mate said, "Hell, no, you can see that light forty or fifty miles on a clear night. Why, I've seen the time you could still see Devil's Island light when we were sixty miles away."

To which I replied, "Well, maybe *you* can, but you don't really see the light in a straight line. The reason why you can see it at that distance is the refraction over the water. It's a sort of a mirage." And I added something about the curvature of the earth.

"Where do you get that hogwash?" he snorted. "Refraction! Cripe, where you been all these years? Curvature! Why, hell's bells, anybody knows that Lake Superior is flat as a pancake. Sure, the earth is curved, but up here on this lake it's perfectly straight!"

A hot argument ensued, which took up a goodly part of the watch, neither side giving any ground. A little later, the mate's wife, who was taking the trip with him, appeared in the wheelhouse. She had for years heard her husband talk about his duties on the freighter, and once on board she had determined to stand every watch with him, to see just what the routine was. She quickly joined the argument.

"Flat?" she exclaimed. "Of course it's flat! Anyone can see that water is flat. All you have to do is pour water in a pan and look at it. Anybody knows it's as level as the floor." With that I subsided, but I was unconvinced.

Tall, spare, with sandy hair and a lean face, this third mate, Bob Kutz, was an understanding officer and a fine shipmate. Each watch, after an hour or two had passed, he would walk over to the wheel and remark, "All right, get away from that wheel now and let me take her. You better stretch your legs and get some exercise."

And then he would tell me to go ahead and navigate the

ship while he steered. So I took bearings on various lights to fix the ship's position, plotting the position and course on the chart. This gave a welcome rest from the long hours at the wheel, which sometimes got painfully tiresome, especially in the night watches in the open lake. It became a sort of a game—the two of us trying to see which one could forecast most accurately the time when the steamer would pass a certain light or would arrive at the Soo, or some port. Once in a while I won, but most of the time the mate won.

In computing the distance the ship would be off a certain light when it was abreast, he used a slide rule. My curiosity was aroused—particularly because I noticed he didn't bother to wait for a bow and beam bearing (45 degrees and 90 degrees) but rather would take bearings from any odd angle that presented itself at the moment—and I accordingly asked what the procedure was. It had been given to him by a member of the Temporary Coast Guard Reserve who had spent a couple of weeks on the *McGean* during the second World War.

1. Set the hair line to the time run between bearings on the A scale.

2. Determine the difference between the first and second angles, and set this difference on the S scale under the hair line.

3. Move the hair line over to the first angle off the S scale.

4. Under the hair line, read on the A scale the time off at second bearing.

5. Move 90 on the S scale under the hair line.

6. Move the hair line over to the second angle off on the S scale.

7. On the A scale, read the time (distance in minutes) you will be off the point of bearing when abeam.

Example

Assume the first bearing to be 30 degrees.
Assume the second bearing to be 45 degrees.
Assume the time between bearings to be 10 minutes.

1. Set the hair line to 10 on the A scale.
2. Slide 15 on the S scale under the hair line.
3. Move the hair line over the first angle on the S scale—30 degrees.
4. On the A scale, read 19.35 minutes, the time off at second bearing.
5. Slide 90 on the S scale under the hair line.
6. Move the hair line to 45 on the S scale.
7. On the A scale, read the time off when abeam—13.6 minutes.

It looked like a lot of work to me—it would be a whole lot simpler to use Table 7 in Bowditch! And the number of steps involved would multiply the possibilities for error.

On a vessel not equipped with radar, fog is serious, causing a lot of gray hair. The radio direction finder is of considerable aid, though it is of no use in the many restricted narrow channels on the lakes because there are no stations along the rivers for broadcasting signals, and even if there were, the accuracy of the bearing would not be close enough to prevent a grounding. Some of the channels are no more than two or three hundred feet wide, and some are no more than a mile long.

In the open lake, however, the radio direction finder is of great value as an aid to fixing a ship's position. Generally speaking, it is a rule that the direction finder is not accurate within two degrees. And yet on many occasions I watched the mate take a bearing on a lightship in thick weather, and upon reaching the vicinity of the lightship, it would appear dead ahead, on the nose.

When approaching a lightship on a radio beacon, the mate will be very careful not to run down the lightship, or Texas Tower, or other aid. The classic example of the danger of collision occurred in May 1934, when the *Olympic*, following the radio beacon of the *Nantucket* lightship, on a course for New York, ran down the lightship, with the loss of four lives.

In thick weather on the lakes, pilots made frequent use of the radio direction finder, fixing the ship's position by taking cross bearings on two different stations, or by use of a single bearing together with the distance-finding signal. In this latter situation, the shore station or lightship sounds an audible code signal simultaneously with the radio signal, and all that is necessary is to count the number of seconds between the two signals, which difference, divided by 5, gives the distance off in statute miles. (Piloting on the lakes is worked with the statute mile as the unit of distance, rather than the nautical mile used on salt water, where the multiplier is 5.5.)

When steering a ship in a fog, I often passed the time at the wheel by counting elephants to determine the number of seconds between the radio and the audible signal, computing the distance thus: one elephant, two elephants, three elephants—a fairly accurate method of counting seconds. The volume control on the radio direction finder is usually turned up very loud, so that the radio signal from the earphones can be heard screaming all through the pilothouse.

Whitefish Bay, an hour's run above the Soo, is twenty-four miles across, a fairly restricted stretch of water, a graveyard of ships. Many vessels have been sunk here in collisions. Matter of fact, the *Superior City*, on which I was ticketed to ship out in April, was sunk here in Whitefish Bay on August 20,

The *Superior City* was built in 1898 in Lorain, Ohio. It sank August 20, 1920, after colliding with Str. *Willis L. King* in Whitefish Bay, Lake Superior, claiming twenty-nine of the thirty-three people aboard, including one passenger. (Photo courtesy of the Great Lakes Historical Society.)

1920, in a collision with the *Willis L. King*. The boilers exploded, killing twenty-nine men. My good fortune, perhaps, that I'd been shifted over to the *Poe* that April.

As a result of these accidents, the Lake Carriers' Association prescribed separate up- and downbound courses to follow, about two miles apart. As on Lake Huron and Lake Superior, the upbound course is on the left, or southerly side of the channel.

I can tell you, it is great to have officers who know exactly where the ship is. One morning, I was at the wheel as the *McGean* followed the course upbound from Point Iroquois in a heavy fog. There was a chorus of steamer whistles all about, but the mate didn't hesitate, though he had the freighter checked somewhat in her speed. Approaching within ten miles of Whitefish Point, he used the radio direction finder continuously, meanwhile keeping track of the distance from the point as the ship neared the lighthouse. As she drew closer to the lighthouse—three miles, two miles, one mile—the bearing kept changing, until finally it read ninety degrees, which is directly abeam. At the same time, the distance signal placed the ship about one mile off the lighthouse, which meant she was less than half a mile off the sandy point. At that moment, the fog lifted, showing the buoy right abreast and about two hundred or three hundred feet to port. The mate knew, with confidence and certainty, exactly where the vessel was at all times. There was no doubt about it at all. As big as these ships are, in these huge lakes they are only minnows. And to control your position that close in the dark is threading a needle blindfolded.

This sort of navigation, however, has all been changed by radar. My first experience with radar was on the *John T. Hutchinson* in a fog going up the Detroit River. Although the visibility was only two or three hundred feet, the radar screen showed a clear outline of the river, plainly depicting the shoreline on both sides and all islands and buoys—even spar buoys—as well as other vessels, in all directions. It is exactly like a map or chart of the vicinity—adjustable to any range from a half a mile to forty miles, with the ship at its center. Ships, buoys, small boats, stakes—these show up as white spots or pips on the radarscope. In most cases, you don't know what they are, but you know there is something there, and you know whether it is moving or standing still. The pilot has in his mind a picture of where each buoy should be, and he recognizes them instantly from their positions on the radarscope. Other objects that are moving are watched with special caution.

The captain invited me to look in the radarscope, while the first mate took the wheel. It was a revelation. It practically eliminates danger from fog, so long as the radar is working properly. In heavy rain or snow, however, there is apt to be some interference, and a heavy sea may produce on the scope a "sea return," which injects an element of uncertainty.

Again, on Lake Erie one watch, about ten miles off Ashtabula on the course for Erie, I watched the radar in operation. The visibility was about three miles. The radar, on a twenty-mile range, plainly showed the shoreline and the breakwater piers of Ashtabula Harbor in their correct outline as on a chart. Two white dots were identified, from the concentric rings on the radarscope, as being some manner of vessels about eight and ten miles, respectively, almost dead ahead. In a few minutes, a large steamer appeared out of the fog ahead and slightly to starboard; and a little later, the other dot showed itself as a small fish tug a point on the port bow.

The radar hasn't taken all the danger out of piloting a ship, but it has eliminated a great deal of it.

Nevertheless, most of the mates with whom I have had the privilege of wheeling still use the time-honored method of the "bow-and-beam" bearing (sometimes known as the "four-point" bearing) for determining how far the ship is off any given point, lighthouse, or what have you. The weakness in the use of the four-point bearing is that the second bearing is taken when you are abreast, and you might be aground by that time. I have never seen any officer use the "double-angle" procedure, or the seven-tenths rule (that is, you take bearings at 22½ degrees and 45 degrees two points and four points, and seven-tenths of the distance run is the estimated distance you will be off the light when it is abeam).

Another device for determining the distance off is the echo. There are not many places where it can be used on the lakes—it requires a perpendicular cliff or bluff. One day, in the North Channel of Georgian Bay, I was awakened in my berth on the little Canadian passenger ferry *Normac* by a blast of the whistle, and pretty soon I heard the echo, and I realized the captain was using the echo (there was a pea-soup fog) to determine how far off he was. He no sooner heard the echo than he rang for full speed ahead, and in fifteen minutes there was the dock at Richards Landing dead ahead.

ON WATCH AT THE WHEEL

In my early days, I put in a trip on the C. G. *Breitung* as an oiler. That and my boyhood exposures gave me a love for the machinery that makes the ships go. Often, when off watch, I was down in the engine room watching the crossheads so smoothly and silently bobbing up and down, or watching the cranks and eccentrics flying around, throwing water on their eighty revolutions a minute. Here in this cave of shining, polished steel and brass and spotless white paint, I frequently spent a half-hour after my watch before turning in, chatting with the engineer or the oiler, asking questions about indicated horsepower, cutoff, vacuum, ballast pumps, siphons, thrust bearings, generators, and the hundreds of machines that clutter the engine room.

On a fine morning watch at the wheel of the *Col. James M. Schoonmaker*, I wondered aloud to the second mate how far the trailing edge of the rudder travels in the arc of its full swing from hard-over port to hard-over starboard. That led to the further inquiry into how far the rudder traveled for each degree of the electric rudder indicator in the wheelhouse. The discussion hadn't progressed very far before it was evident that one must know the length of the rudder—measured from the center of the rudder pin to the trailing edge—in order to compute the answer. So at dinner that noon in the dining room, I put it to John Mansiki, the chief engineer. "How long is the rudder?" The chief didn't know, but he would find out. (A fine gentleman, John Mansiki later lost his life after falling into the cargo hold of the *Wm. P. Snyder.*)

Dinner over, I strolled forward to go on watch at the wheel. Not ten minutes later, the telephone rang. It was the chief's voice. "The length of the rudder from the center of the pin to the extreme after edge is seven and a half feet."

At supper, the discussion was renewed among the second mate, myself, and the chief engineer. And then the waiter got into it. He was a teacher of math in the Cleveland schools, working his summer vacation on the steamboats. The solution was soon found. Assuming that the rudder is hard over at forty-five degrees, the distance traveled from hard over to hard over would be approximately $90 \times 1.5708 = 141.37$ inches, or about twelve feet. It wasn't possible to turn the wheel a little and have the rudder move one degree. When the wheel is turned perhaps as much as a half a turn, it merely takes up the slack in the chain of cables, gears, and/or shafting between the wheel and the steering engine in the fantail—nearly six hundred feet away. Even with an electric steering gear, there is a small amount of play—perhaps a spoke or two. As soon as the slack is taken up and the wheel is turned just a hair farther, the steering engine will turn the rudder two or three degrees before it stops. Accordingly, when the wheel is turned enough to actuate the rudder, the rudder will move from three to six inches one way or the other. And this is the reason it is so difficult to put the vessel on a perfectly straight course which she will follow without the necessity of moving the wheel.

By careful attention to steering, it is possible to move the rudder to one side just enough to meet the ship's swing, and then bring it back to dead center, so that the ship will stay on her course for a few minutes at a time. And once in a long time, with proper conditions of wind and a light ship, and with great concentration, she can be put on her course and will keep it for half an hour, or even an hour or more—but these instances are rare.

Another idiosyncrasy of a steamship is the tendency for the rudder to "creep," which means that when you have turned the wheel a spoke or two, the rudder indicator pointer will move to about where you want it, and then when you take your eye off the indicator for a moment to look at the compass or out the window at a passing vessel perhaps, the steering engine will slowly turn over another revolution or so, and the rudder will creep another degree or two. This is very baffling and annoying and makes it necessary to give much closer attention to the electric rudder indicator than otherwise might be the case. It is a trouble that is almost impossible to cure, for if the valve adjustment on the steering engine is set up too fine, the springing and bouncing of the vessel throughout her length will open up the valve now and then and cause the rudder to turn without any movement of the wheel at all.

It was possible for me, in the old days, steering by magnetic compass, to cover up my erratic steering—which is characteristic of all wheelsmen while steering in the open lake, because it is tiring and nerve-racking to maintain continually an intense concentration on steering the ship within, say, half a degree of her course. A four-hour stretch at the wheel steering in the rivers is vastly more tiring than in the lakes. As a result, the wheelsman will permit the ship to yaw from her course from time to time as much as a degree or perhaps even two. (And once in a while, when the pilothouse talk gets very interesting, she may go off three or four degrees—but this is bad steering, and a wheelsman who lets that happen may get at the least a good ribbing from the mate.) This doesn't mean that the ship will be delayed at all in arriving at her destination. You have the choice of two evils. If you steer to a fine hair and hold her within a half a degree, you will use more rudder, which in turn will slow the ship down. On the other hand, if you permit the ship to swing a little bit more, she will actually travel a little farther, but she will travel faster, because you are not using so much rudder. A good wheelsman will compensate the ship's course by letting her work off to one side for a few minutes and then let her work back to the other side for a while.

But even in the open lake, there is a time when you must, or should, steer very accurately—within one click of the gyro compass, which is equivalent to one-sixth of a degree, for the gyro repeater emits a faint *click* six times for each degree the lubber mark moves on the compass card. Such a time is when the mate is taking a bearing on a light.

To everyone who has the barest smattering of trigonometry, it is apparent that a difference of half a degree in the ship's heading when you are taking a bearing will produce a very appreciable error in the estimated distance off the light. On a distance run of ten miles, an error of one degree in the compass reading will produce an error of approximately one-sixth of a mile in the calculated distance. Of course, this wouldn't cut much ice if the ship were going to be five or ten miles off a dangerous spot in passing; but if she is only going to be half a mile or a mile off when the light is abreast, especially if the weather is thick, it's a very nice thing to know just exactly how far off you will be. The rule for the wheelsman is to keep her right on the mark when the mate is taking a bearing; and if you *do* happen to be off your course a little, say so. The mate will respect you for it.

Approaching a light at night, the mate is watching through the bearing finder, and as soon as the light is in line with the slots or wires, he calls out, "How is she now?"

And in former days, when you steered by magnetic compass and there was no gyro to keep you on your toes, I was wont to reply that I was right on the mark, when as a matter of fact I might have been a half a degree, or a whole degree, or possibly even as much as two degrees off. And this is extremely bad, for it produced an error in the calculated distance off and might conceivably result in running the ship on the rocks. Having been caught in the deception two or three times, I quickly learned to tell the truth about it. Always, as soon as the mate prepared to take a bearing, it was time to steady the ship on her course, and it became a matter of pride to have the ship exactly on the course when the mate sang out. But if, as sometimes happened, the ship would start to swing off just at that critical moment (steamships are very perverse, which is perhaps why they are called "she"), I learned to swallow my pride and say, "She's two clicks to the right." Even if she were a whole degree off, the only safe thing is to tell the mate about it and permit him to correct his bearing accordingly.

Editor's Note: From this point, Mr. Dutton's story abandons normal chronology. Events having certain philosophical commonalty, despite time disparity, group themselves. Thus, the story moves freely backward and forward in time. But you know how it is with helmsmen—the more frequent the wheel adjustments, the truer the course.

Dutton here shows us a few things about steering a ship or a life.

CHAPTER VII

NIGHT THOUGHTS

ON THE SOO RIVER

There's something about sailing the Soo river country!

And there's something more about having the experience under your belt so you can relax and enjoy it!

Even the routine navigation is music.

Lightning flared the lower St. Marys River, lighting up the fuel dock at Detour and momentarily blinding me. Holding course as the skipper rang for half speed, then slow, I adjusted my steering to the *McGean's* loss of headway. The thunderstorm held off, though it looked to be upon us any minute. Her bow was abreast of the coal dock now. The captain turned the engine-room telegraph to full astern, and the wheelhouse shook from the reversed engines. I put the rudder amidships. The skipper stepped out the port door to watch over the side as the steamer swung in to lie alongside the dock. Then he stuck his head into the wheelhouse.

"Stop those engines!"

I turned the Chadburn to stop, watching the answering

The pilothouse telegraph, which the captain uses to signal the chief engineer. (Alan W. Sweigert photo.)

pointer for the engineer's confirmation. I went below to the winches, stopping by my room long enough to get my work gloves and slicker just as the storm struck.

Half an hour later, the ship fueled, I was back at the wheel. The deckhands had come aboard, the lines were cast off, the freighter pulled away from the coal dock, and I headed her to the right of the midchannel buoy off Lime Island which flashed its short-long dimly through the rain. As the vessel came abreast of Lime Island, heading north, the storm moved off to the south and the sky cleared. The moon shone softly on black water—another fine night on the river. Nature is nowhere more prodigal with her splendors than in the Soo river country.

As I hauled westward at Pte. Aux Frenes and came around to head on the Winter Point Range, ten miles across Mud Lake, I noted a big freighter coming up astern. Another ship passed downbound, to port, silent except for a faint sighing of steam. She was beautiful with her lights shining on the water.

Half an hour more, and we were almost across Mud Lake. The steamer coming up astern was hauling abreast, having blown one blast for permission to pass to starboard.

"Let her come right now, Fred." The captain spoke the order softly, as he blew one blast, permission to pass.

I put the wheel a full turn right and looked aft to watch the smokestack start around. The big stranger was taking the inside of the turn, close to the buoy. The two ships raced along, side by side. I kept alert not to get too close, and I pictured the other wheelsman doing the same.

"Slow," came the order, and I spun the wheel a couple turns left to slow her swing, then amidships before she stopped swinging altogether. Letting her turn slowly, I kept one eye on the passing freighter, which was drawing ahead now. The bow of the *McGean* came within a hundred feet of the other fellow's fantail.

"Steady her there, now, Fred," the captain ordered. "Follow the other steamer." I gave her a little left wheel again to stop the swing and steadied her when the steering pole lined up on the middle of the bunch of lights that was the other steamer.

Pretty soon, I saw the steamer ahead begin to swing left at Johnson Point. I noted the compass course—017 degrees—and almost immediately the lights of the Sailors' Encampment Range appeared ahead as the lead steamer pulled to the left. You watch that when the skipper gives you the order to follow the steamer ahead at night. So long as the other ship holds the same course, you can keep steering on him, but as soon as he turns, you had better not follow him. You'll end up in the woods or among the cows in a pasture. Don't cut cross lots in these rivers. As long as you keep watching your compass courses, you will be all right. And steer on the ranges. If the other steamer's smoke hides the range lights, you have the compass. You can steer by compass even in the narrowest channels. And in the fog, the compass absolutely saves you from parking the ship on some village green, air strip, football field, or post office.

We were coming up pretty close on the range now, and I kept an eye on the quick-flash buoy to port, waiting for the order to make that turn. As the ship came abreast of the buoy, the skipper called, "You can left now, Fred," and I started her around, looking aft at the smokestack again.

"Put her on the range," came the next order.

It was always a kind of game with a wheelsman, to see how close he could come to bringing the range lights over the stern, right in line, without increasing or slowing the swing of the steamer. If you got her swinging too fast, you'd

Emergency steering wheel. A gang of crewmen operates it by muscle power in the event of a malfunction of the steering engine. (Alan W. Sweigert photo.)

miss it and have to work her over some more; but if you let her swing too slowly, you'd miss it on the far side and have to coax her back.

Soon the Rains Wharf Range was closing up astern on the starboard quarter. I could see she was getting over a little too far, so I gave her some more left to make her swing faster. The stern was almost there now, the range lights closing up rapidly. I met her with a half a turn of right wheel, and the range lights came in line, one over the other just as the smokestack swung in line. I steadied the ship then and steered facing the range astern for a time.

It's a great sensation.

The Point of Woods Range was ahead on the same course, and Captain Kristiansen told me to steer on it. The next turn was only a mile away—a five-minute run. Here was the Dark Hole, well named. Black as pitch. When you're in the dark, stick to basics. You are all right so long as you stay on the ranges. In no time, the quick-flash buoy was abreast, and I swung the freighter to the right again.

It was always fine to steer a steamship up the St. Marys River on a dark, clear night—an exhilarating thing. Tonight it was at its best. A small north breeze rippled the water, humming in the rigging. The moon was setting over the dark pines to the west, while the northern lights flung their eerie banners flaring the northern sky. All else was dark, except for the line of buoys blinking on either side and the brilliant gleam of the range lights ahead and astern. You felt as though you were in another world. It was strong wine.

On a night like that, you think back over what you learned in steamboating, and from whom. One of the important things I had learned was from a blue heron and a miserable first mate.

OLE—MASTER AFTER GOD

Back when I was a young ordinary seaman, we had Ole, the meanest first mate I ever had. He was sadistic and took out his hatred of life on the deckhands. He considered himself quite an old-time bucko mate and next after God. His orders were always bellowed and salted with obscene curses. No matter what we did, he was never satisfied. He kept himself in a state of continual rage. He hated the skipper for his soft ways and superior position; and, not daring to show it, he took it out on the deckhands.

He would call us out to soogey the cabins, but the skipper would turn us in again and tell Ole that the ship didn't need soogeying that trip. The mate attempted to work us on Sunday, but the captain wouldn't stand for it unless it was necessary for the safety of the ship.

So Ole's hatred for the skipper grew and festered, and the more it grew, the more he rode the deckhands. He would make us do unnecessary jobs, excoriating us with foul words for no reason but to stay in practice.

I left my oilskin slicker on the fantail one night. When I went back later, it was gone. One of the oilers told me the mate had tossed it overboard.

On another occasion, Mike, the little Irish deck watch, had some bluebells planted in a tin can. He had dug them up on Presque Isle at Marquette and was carrying them home to Cleveland for his mother. He had watered the flowers and tended them carefully all the way down the lakes. The Centurion was lying at anchor in Cleveland Harbor, and Mike was waiting at the rail for the supply boat to take him ashore. He had the can with the flowers resting on the rail as he held it in his hand.

Ole spied the flowers. "Vat de hell you doin' wit da posies, huh?"

"Taking them to my mother," Mike replied.

"Yah, you big sissy! Flowers to your mama?" The mate playfully struck the wooden rail with his thick hand, and the can of flowers jumped overboard. Mike's eyes filled with tears of rage.

I knew that someday my turn would come to get point-blank crossways with this mate, and what would I do about it? I wondered. How would I conduct myself?

On the way down Lake Superior one clear, warm August afternoon, a large blue heron flew aboard the ship and perched on a hatch amidships. It was several miles from the nearest shore and was evidently exhausted from its flight. From the wheelhouse, the captain, the second mate, and I watched as three of the deckhands approached the big, un-gainly bird and surrounded it. Closing in on it, one of the sailors made a rush and clutched it to his breast. But he quickly let go, for the bird turned its head and attacked him with its beak. The deckhands backed away completely. After an hour, the heron, rested, flew away.

I was impressed with the way that heron handled life's bullies.

A few days later, the *Centurion* was entering Racine Harbor, heavily laden with coal. Rain dumped out of the clouds, and the night was black. The deckhands stood under the break of the Texas cabin to keep out of the downpour. Suddenly, the sound of the rain driving across the deck was pierced.

The "Whaleback" was the first radically new bulk carrier design since Captain Peck first crowded the pilothouse forward on top of the bow and moved the engine aft, leaving uncluttered access to cargo holds. The purpose of the whale shape was to shed water, snow, and wind. It did. Thirty-nine were built and operated with great success for many years. The last whaleback operating on the lakes was the *Meteor*, converted to an oil tanker. She ran late into the danger seasons on Lake Michigan before being decommissioned.

104

"Get dat blasted ladder over!" came Ole's order. The bull-shaped mate was wrestling with the heavy ladder. Silently, the deckhands helped him lift it and swing one end over the wire rail. The *Centurion* touched the dock with a slight tremble. Down went the lower end of the ladder to the dock, unseen below in the gloom.

"Down on the dock, you lazy bastids! An' take a heavin' line. Slim, what de hell you waitin' for?"

Over the side I went, a formless shape in the murk, bundled up in oilskins, my face hidden under a sou'wester hat. Carefully, I felt my way down the ladder, rung to rung. Still there was no sound but the hissing of the rain.

This was in the days before the landing boom and the floodlight.

The ladder was wobbly and unsteady. I was near the bottom now. I felt for the dock with my foot, stepping off the last rung, and I felt myself falling. There was a splash. I hit the water. "Man overboard!" roared Captain Bradshaw from up on the bridge. I had fallen through a gaping hole in the dock, landing on my back in the water six feet below dock level.

Terrified, thrashing about in the black, slimy water, my hand caught a dock stringer. I pulled myself along it until my feet touched the sloping bottom, and I crawled up the plank and climbed out onto the dock. I poured the water out of my boots. The rasping voice of the mate battered me from the deck. "Dammit, what de holy hell you tank you doin' own there? You OK?"

"Yeah. I'm OK," I growled back. But the blue heron was in my mind. This was my time. The mate had no business sending a man down the ladder without making certain it was safe, even if this was before the days of the landing boom and the floodlight.

106

The sopping coil of heavy line dropped around my ears. Grabbing it, I hauled the steel cable across the dock and dropped it around a spile, then repeated the operation with the other three cables, fore and aft. When the ship was moored, I coiled up the dripping line and yelled up to the deck, "Mate!"

When I saw by his silhouette against the murky sky that I had his attention, I yelled, *"This is for you!"*

With perhaps the biggest physical effort of my life, I took careful aim and swung the heavy coil with all my might up at his silhouette. My aim was true, and the heavy wet line smacked the mate across the face.

The profane outburst was music to my ears, and I added, "That was no accident!"

I climbed aboard. Like the blue heron, I rested. Then I walked right past the mate to my room to change into dry clothes.

I never had any trouble with Ole after that . . . or with any of the Oles in my life.

AT THE WHEEL WITH A NEW MAN

It is surprising how experience forgets the awesome fright of the first few times at the wheel of a steamboat. Or any big responsibility. I forgot until upbound in the Middle Neebish Rock Cut. One night on the old *Colonel*, the skipper turned over the ship to the second mate. Soon Al, the deck watch, brought the coffeepot, cups, sugar, and a can of cow. We were in Hay Lake, above Neebish Island.

"Want to hold her for a while?" I asked Al.

"Me? In the rivers? Hell, no!"

"Why not?" I countered. "You'll have to learn to steer in the rivers sooner or later."

"Oh, no, not me."

The mate chimed in, "Go ahead, Al. We're in Hay Lake. There's a lot of room."

"All right," Al conceded dubiously. "But you better keep an eye on it so I don't pile her on the rocks." And he took the wheel while I poured the coffee.

"Gee, this is easy enough," Al spoke up. "It's just like steering in the lake."

"Sure, nothing to it," I said. "Only . . . when we get up to the locks, you want to be careful not to hit the wall too hard."

"Hey, what is this?" Al panicked. "You take her. I ain't taking the steamboat into no locks."

"Go on, I was kidding. You hold her for a while, and when we get up in the Little Rapids Cut I'll relieve you."

"OK, but no funny business."

So Al steered the freighter up the river, gaining confidence by the mile. The talk continued about steering, and I said something about having to be quick sometimes in a narrow place.

An approaching downbound steamer showed a bright flash of lights on her foremast. The watchman's voice was heard from the fo'c'sle. "Blows one whistle!"

"Blows one," repeated the second mate, and they heard the distant boom of the steamer's whistle. The second mate moved over to the whistle pull and blew an answering blast, first opening a valve and pumping a lever two or three strokes.

"Let her work a couple of degrees to the right, Al. Give that fellow a little more room to pass." Al put the wheel over a couple of spokes and then steadied her up.

"Handy sort of gadget you've got there," I commented, as I noticed the mate fiddling with the valve.

"Hell of an inconvenient gadget, if you ask me," replied the second mate. "Damn engineers. They don't give a mate

Passing whalebacks commanded attention from all boat crews. (Photo courtesy of the Dutton Collection.)

credit for knowing anything. This fool thing—every once in a while, you have to pump it up, or else it won't blow the whistle. Leaks pressure. Hell's bells, they won't buy any new equipment for this wagon. Last spring, I rigged up an electric whistle lever. Worked fine. But when the chief engineer discovered it, he ripped it out and put back this blasted hydraulic affair."

Al was hearing none of this. His eyes were drilling the other vessel. I knew he was thinking no river is wide enough for two of these monsters to pass.

"Let her come over now on the range lights, Al," the mate said, for the downbound steamer was abreast.

109

Al's voice was parched. "Come and take this thing!" As the ship neared the narrowing channel, Al felt he was threading a needle with a clothesline. "Take it!" In fact, she *had* suddenly begun to steer sluggishly.

I took the wheel. "She *is* dragging her tail some," I noted. "That damned second assistant engineer must be blowing flues again. Every watch just about this time, she starts to slow down and steers like a scow. Bet you she isn't making more than six miles an hour. I raised hell with him about it the other night, and I think he does it on purpose just to get my goat. Likes to do it just when we are coming to a tight spot where I need all the power I can get for steering. The other night, he pulled it on me coming down past the lightship above Port Huron. There I was trying to keep her straight in a following sea, and the water shoaling under us, and that jackass lets the pressure go down. Hardly had any steerageway at all. I thought I was going to slam her right down on the beach at Port Edward."

"I noticed you were having troubles all right," the second mate said. "It's a wonder the old man puts up with it. I don't know why he doesn't give the chief hell. If I was the skipper, I would."

"Yeah, the skipper knew what was going on all right. He never said a word to me, and she was swinging off a point or more each side of the course. All he said was, 'Keep your shirt on. When she gets in the channel, she'll be going along like a bloomin' racehorse.' "

"Let her come left now, Fred," the mate said. "You can head her right up on the green range lights." I put the wheel over, and the steamer came around slowly. The mate and I just might have been laying it on some for the benefit of Al, who was all ears. He went below to sound the tanks, like a man escaping.

"And the skipper was right," I continued. "When I swung her around on the range at Fort Gratiot, he had her turning up full speed again, and she steered fine, and with the current in the river she was going along like a damn express train. And the skipper was happy as a lark, and hollering, 'Look at the son of a bitch go!' "

The mate and I were both laughing, and the captain came in, settled himself on his stool in the front window, and started humming a tune as he looked over the situation.

"All right, Fred," he said after a few minutes, "You can bend her around to the right now."

So I brought her around to the right and headed her on the buoy at the far end of the Little Rapids Cut. The first mate came in with a bright "Good morning," followed by his wheelsman, and the watch was ended. I passed the word to the other wheelsman that she was heading on the buoy, and I surrendered the wheel.

Red, the watchman, was sitting at the mess-room table over a cup of coffee as the second mate and I entered. "We'll be at the Soo in half an hour," Red remarked.

"Yes, and a beautiful night to go ashore," I commented.

"Fat chance you'll get to go ashore, with the locks swarming with soldiers. They only let two deckhands on the wall, and that's all."

"Seems to me I saw the first mate get off to go to the lock office last trip."

"Mates and captains don't count. When I missed the boat at Marquette a couple trips ago, maybe you think I didn't have myself a time convincing the army that I should get aboard at the Soo. I got an order from the Coast Guard, but the army didn't want to let me pass anyway. Why don't those guys get together?"

The whalebacks were designed by Alexander McDougall. (Photo courtesy of the Dutton Collection.)

The talk ebbed and flowed. It was the best time of the night, in the mess hall when you came off watch and could relax over a cup of coffee. Under all the small lies flying about lay a few giant truths.

AT THE DOCK

It was two A.M. The ship was nearly loaded, and I, with the third mate and the watchman, sat idly discussing the weather. As we talked, we saw a light line dropping down from the top of the towering ore dock, seventy feet above. On the end of the line was a workman's glove, limp and stained with iron ore dust. We watched the first mate go over to the glove and put something in it. As soon as he did this, the glove rose back up, dancing and twisting on the end of the line, until it was lifted out of sight by a workman

112

up there on the dim height of the dock. The ore shoots came down.

"Those fellows have to have their beer money," explained the third mate, "or they wouldn't give us a good load."

"Curious sort of racket," I commented.

"Started a long time ago," the mate said. "Never get a quick load if you didn't give them a few bucks. There'd be all kinds of delays. It's like tipping a waiter in a restaurant. Only here the tip comes first . . . or you'll get poor service. It doesn't come out of the mate's pocket; it's charged against the ship. Those ore punchers up there put it in a kitty, and every so often they throw a party uptown somewhere. Amounts to quite a piece of change, when you consider they load maybe ten or fifteen vessels in a day sometimes at this one dock."

And the three of us sat silent for a while, I musing on how this tip was listed on the company books. I'd seen the glove on a rope many times and marveled. Nothing is ever said—just the soiled and tattered glove dropping down out of the sky. Then it goes up, and the ore chutes come down.

The skipper's wife was aboard while the ship lay at the ore dock. They lived in Duluth and saw each other almost every trip, though only for an hour or two. Often, when his ship came in, she was on the dock waiting for him—a lonely figure standing there, looking unbelievably small and frail against the background of the immense ore dock structure that towered above her.

Finally, the ten thousand tons of red iron ore were in the hold; the ship was properly trimmed all around. The breast lines came in.

The captain's wife went down the ladder, following him

for safety. The loaded steamer's rail was only a few feet above the lower level of the dock now. The skipper said good-bye to his wife, speaking to her with an air of embarrassed disinterest, for the crew was watching. In a moment, he turned and climbed back aboard, calling to the mate as he mounted the companionway to the fo'c'sle deck.

"OK, Tom, we can go now."

I followed up the companionway to the wheelhouse and stood ready at the wheel. The skipper took a quick look out the door and darted back to the Chadburn, twisting the handle down to full astern. Then he blew a short blast on the big whistle—the signal to cast off. The tug at the steamer's bow panted and breathed fire as it began its mighty David-and-Goliath shoving. The freighter moved slowly astern. Then a long blast of the whistle, warning other ships.

The wheel was amidships as I stood there ready for the order which I knew would not come until the engines stopped backing. You always keep your rudder amidships while your engines are going astern. It wouldn't do any good to turn the wheel, for the rudder has no effect in steering a large freighter moving astern, and it would put a strain on the rudder and the quadrant.

In the gathering dusk, I saw again the skipper's pretty wife standing on the dock beside a bollard. So diminutive she looked, so alone—a tiny spot of white on the gigantic dock. She raised a hand in farewell; her pretty features showed a ghost of a wistful smile.

The skipper appeared not to notice her. His love for her was evident enough, even though captains work at covering their emotions in front of the crew. I felt like saying, "Go on and wave to her."

As the vessel backed out past the end of the dock, the white figure grew smaller and smaller. Then she was gone.

114

CHAPTER VIII

SHIPMATES

Editor's Note: In addition to the human interplay, one of the values of this Dutton manuscript is recording for future readers the nuts-and-bolts detail of how things were done before self-unloaders, diesels, bowthrusters, and gyro-compasses.

LOADING

With the longer spouts on the docks in the new era, they will load sixteen, eighteen, or even twenty-five thousand tons of iron ore into a freighter in three to six hours, and all the deckhands do is get on the dock now and then, handling the lines four or five times as the steamship is moved along the dock for another run.

The pockets in the dock hold about three hundred fifty tons of ore each. As soon as the steamer is tied up to the dock, one set of alternate spouts is let down; it looks as though it were going to drill right through the bottom of the ship. Up goes a door at the bottom of the pocket, and then down comes the ore with a rush, accompanied by a hissing and an occasional bang and thump as large chunks of ore hit the side tank. In a few minutes, the ore has run out, except for a little stuck along the sides of the pockets which is chipped and scraped out by the ore punchers perched up there on their narrow dark platforms. Once in a long while, one of these men will lose his footing and slide into the hold of the steamship. If he is lucky, he will not be buried in the heavy ore or struck on the head by a chunk. On deck, you stay out of the way. Stray pebbles of ore fly onto the deck, and you don't want to get hit with even a pebble-sized piece. Iron ore is heavy. They can load a ship way up to her decks with coal, but only something less than half full of ore.

As soon as the first-run pockets are empty, there will come a shout from the first mate, responsible for loading and trimming the ship. "Let her go ahead. Deckhands on dock!"

The wheelsman forward and the third mate or perhaps the bos'n or the watchman aft, will start the valves or controllers on the steam or electric winches, and the great vessel will start to move along the dock.

One of the men at the rail watches the splice in the end of the steel cable so that it doesn't get so short (or nearly up and down) that it flies off the bollard. Somebody could get hurt. Veteran deckhands stand clear of the cables on the dock. As soon as the cable is getting dangerously short in his judgment, the man at the rail yells to the wheelsman, "Stick out," at the same time making that hand signal to stop heaving, and then another signal to stick out on the line.

Strange expression. How can anyone "stick out" a limp steel cable? The old Indian rope trick?

The wheelsman yanks the reverse lever and cuts down the steam. The cable unwinds fast, and the wheelsman, busy now as a beaver, jumps around the winch and starts pulling out the cable so that it doesn't tangle up on the drum. He can't stick out on it—he must pull it out. A hundred feet or so of cable run out, while the deckhand is toiling along the dock dragging it behind him; the mate shouts at him, "Drop it on that one!" He signals the wheelsman to heave in; the wheelsman reverses the winch and gives it the steam again, watching the mate's hand like a hawk all the time, for he must keep in mind the safety of that deckhand on the dock. As soon as the slack is nearly taken up, the mate's hand is held up flat out, as if for silence, and the wheelsman shuts the juice almost off. When the cable pulls up taut, he gives it the steam again to keep the steamship moving along the dock.

All this sounds easy, but at the same time the wheelsman is going through the same antics with the cable that leads aft along the dock, and he must handle the two winches at once. Meanwhile, on the dock, the deckhand is running back and forth from one cable to the other. In a minute or two comes a yell from the first mate amidships on deck— "Forty-eight feet!"—accompanied by a signal with his two fists held high above his head, and the wheelsman turns the valve and cuts down the steam on the winch which is heaving on the cable leading ahead. That signal means the ship must be stopped when he has moved another forty-eight feet along the dock. The hatches are on twelve- or twenty-four-foot centers. Then "Twenty-four feet" with one hand raised, and the wheelsman opens the steam on the other winch to check the steamer's way. Then a shout of "Twelve feet!" and, judging how much steam it will take to stop the ship with her hatches neatly centered opposite the proper dock spouts, the wheelsman cuts the steam on the heaving winch still more, meanwhile opening up the valve on the other winch, and all the while watching the first mate, who is moving his hands toward each other in a vertical plane, closer and closer, like a pair of scissors. Quickly the closing hands come together, the mate shouts, "Hang on to her!" And the wheelsman puts a lot of steam on the winch with the cable leading aft, against the momentum of the moving vessel. She grinds to a stop, the cables snapping and cracking in a most alarming manner, but if the wheelsman knows his business, nothing lets go, and the ship is under the spouts exactly where the mate wants it.

Instantly the wheelsman turns a lot of steam into the other winch, so she won't start moving in the other direction. Sometimes maybe she's gone a shade too far, and they pull her back a couple of feet. It's pure artistry how they can pull twenty or twenty-five thousand tons of steamship and cargo back and forth along the dock and stop all that mass right where they want it.

Next, the deckhand runs along the dock toward the bow and the mate tosses him a heaving line. The wheelsman dashes down into the windlass room and sticks out of the breast line, which is another cable on the winch down there in the windlass room. The cable is pulled out by the deckhand and dropped over the bollard, and the wheelsman heaves the ship up against the dock. Another breast line is run out aft. If they didn't use breast lines, the force of the ore plunging into the hold would push the vessel away from the dock.

The spouts are dropped into the hatches; loading continues.

Now I can sit down on a bollard on the dock until it is necessary to move the ship again, or perhaps I climb on deck and curl up in a corner for a nap. Usually four or five moves are all that are needed to load and trim the ship. But night or day, the deckhands must be on deck.

The mate is continually watching the draft marks on the stem and stern post. It is a nice piece of judgment not to let the ship be loaded too deep and at the same time have her trimmed on an even keel as well as fore and aft. He wants her down a little bit by the stern, for she steers best that way; and he keeps in mind that with all that iron ore in her, she'll be five or six inches deeper amidships than she is fore and aft, because of the weight of the ore bending her in the middle like a bow. If he should let her be loaded two or three inches too deep, that would be too bad, for she wouldn't go through the locks at the Soo. He might take a chance on it, but they might have to put her under an unloading dock and lighten her a few hundred tons. No mate can let that happen and expect to hold his job.

You must report your draft to the Coast Guard above the Soo when you pass. You might kid them into believing you were an inch or two lighter than you actually are, but they have binoculars—they can read the draft marks for themselves. No mates can afford having a fat fine slapped against the company and maybe having the Coast Guard refuse to let the ship enter the lock. So the mate is very careful he doesn't let them load her too deep. It's a neat trick, too, putting in that last trimming run of ore. There are three or four hundred tons of iron ore in each pocket up there, and once they open the door, they can't close it again until the ore has run out into the ship. Well, three hundred tons of ore in one end of the steamer will sink her down several inches. They might have half a pocket here and there, but it's close.

In modern times, the iron ore is mostly in the form of pellets. The loading is faster, since the pellets are dry and flow freely under all weather conditions.

The vessels' iron ore customers—the steel mills. This one is the former U.S. Steel Central Furnace, Cuyahoga River, Cleveland, which operated from 1893 to 1978. (Alan W. Sweigert photo.)

SHORE LEAVE

Liquor being forbidden aboard ship, it is natural that when a seaman gets ashore for a few hours during unloading, he heads someplace for a little polite drinking or even a bit of two-handed, down-to-the-gunwales imbibing, just for the fun of it. Then, too, there may be a little serious drinking, but not done seriously; there is a difference.

On one such night, I cashed my paycheck in the Round Bar—it was for $40.39—and received $40.35 in cash. I asked the barmaid about the four cents, and she archly informed me, "We don't give any change under a nickel." Which was all right. Some places charge sailors a dime for cashing a check.

After three or four bottles of beer there, it was time to consider some drinking. At the Crow's Nest, we had a few shots of the high-test goods, and life was really beginning to look good. The third mate suggested it was time to make rounds.

At the Orient, the main style was shots with beer chasers—the old-time boilermakers. This was getting nice. A couple of the lads got a little noisy with some fairly personal-type allusions and had to be escorted to the side-walk by the house gorilla. The rest of us went along, to keep the others out of trouble, of course.

At the Bar Sinister, the crew started drinking liquor in their beer. Then Harry, the fireman, thought it would be more efficient to drink beer in the liquor. This seemed to improve our singing.

Then someone misconstrued, I'm sure, a harmless re-mark. The resulting jambalaya was not at all serious. While there was some swelling and discoloration, most of the blood was only from the watchman's nose. Nevertheless, the proprietor requested the boys seek other accommoda-tions. He held open the door. The watchman, however, once on the street, had an afterthought. "Nobody's going to take a sucker punch at me an' get away with it." But as he charged back in, the door seemed to be stuck shut.

That was not a major inconvenience. Around the cor-ner, still open, was the Hole in the Wall. The watch went in and ordered another round. I was sitting at the bar observ-ing proceedings and minding my own business, and the night was fine and all was well, when from the stool beside me an attractive-looking young woman said, "What boat you from, sailor?"

"*McGean*," I said.

"What do you do on her?"

"Wheelsman."

"You know Jim Johnson, on the *Ashley?*"

"Nope."

"He's nice," the girl confided. "I like wheelsmen." And she sort of hauled closer.

I thought to myself, Hell, there's no more reason to like wheelsmen than any other member of the crew, except, of course, oilers and engineers—especially engineers. I was always suspicious of engineers, such a serious and unimaginative lot. It must be the result of working in that engine room all the time. Can't see out of the ship, and in time they can't see out of their souls. The third mate also took a dim view of engineers. Whenever the third answered the engine-room phone in the pilothouse, he answered, "Brains department," which bent the rapport some.

But I was intrigued by this girl sitting on my port. Blond. Nice lines, if a bit broad in the beam, and heavy on paint. A guy'd certainly get plenty smeared up if he tried to kiss her, I thought. Not much left of the night by that time, and a guy might even get rolled for his money.

But I thought it wouldn't do any harm to talk. Her chatter broke through, "Don't you like rye, wheelsman?"

"Sure, but I like bourbon better." And I ordered a couple of drinks.

"What's your name, wheelsman? I can't go on calling you wheelsman all night, can I?"

"Name's Bill," I replied. "What do you care?"

She pouted. "Now you're being nasty."

I smiled at her.

"Can't we have another drink, Bill?"

"Sure. Bartender, another."

"What do you do when you're out on the ship, Billy boy?"

"Shucks," I came back, "I steer the steamship. And my name ain't Billy boy."

"All right, Bill, I'm sorry. Don't you like me a little?"

"Sure. In fact, you interest me."

"Honest? Tell me about that."

I drew a deep breath and blew aside the alcoholic curtain for a minute. "Well," I said, "it's like this. How do you get into a business like you are in?"

"What do you mean?" After a while, she spoke again. "I don't know. I just guess it had a lot of glamour. Jean, my girlfriend, did pretty good, and I thought it would be swell to have all that spending money. You know—good clothes, shoes, hats. Gee, that's what looked good to me."

"Well," I asked, "how did it pan out? I mean, do you have all those clothes you wanted, and so on?"

The girl looked thoughtful. "Yes, I guess so. Sure, yeah, I make out pretty good at it."

"Well, what about the other side of it?"

"What do you mean?"

"Oh, I just mean about these drinks. I tasted yours; it's only tea. How much of a cut do you get on the drinks?"

She exploded. Clawing hands went for my face. I toppled backwards off the stool. The third mate grabbed the girl to hold her back. Some others got into it. The bartender reached over and stroked the fireman's head with a piece of lumber. Suddenly the air was full of knuckles. A flying barstool leveled the bartender. The McGean staff felt it was time to adjourn the meeting, dragging the fallen fireman.

I suggested a breakfast meeting to revive the wounded. At breakfast, somebody remembered the ship, and that started the crew back toward the dock. Everyone managed the ladder test safely. Once on deck, the fireman produced a bottle of vodka he had acquired and invited everyone to his room for a nightcap.

Over vodka came philosophy . . . as the sun rose.

When the seminar adjourned, the third mate, the watchman, and I made our way forward to turn in. It was four bells—six A.M.—and I had to go on watch at eight o'clock. The ship was practically unloaded and ready to sail when I tumbled into my bunk.

I woke up suddenly and looked at my watch. It was ten A.M. I had a horrible headache. The room turned. Dashing up the companionway, two steps at a time, I burst into the pilothouse and found the third mate gaily steering the ship down Lake Michigan.

"Why didn't you call me?" I took the wheel.

"Hell." The third mate laughed. "I called you for half an hour. I decided you were dead."

The *McGean* took an odd course down Lake Michigan that morning.

Editor's note: Fred Dutton's biography recalls two other interesting shore leaves in sharp contrast.

It was a bitter winter day that Sunday afternoon in late November as the *Willis L. King* lay at the ore dock in Allouez. I was pretty bored with life, for the ship had been lying at the dock a week, loading. The ore was frozen in the dock pockets, and the only way the dock workmen could get it to run into the ship's hold was to dig it out with their long-handled spades, laboriously. I wondered if the vessel would be loaded in time to sail before she was frozen in for the winter. Already there were four inches of ice on the harbor, and more forming as fast as the tugs broke it up. I decided to go over to Duluth to a picture show to break the monotony. Since the *King* had been there a week, she wouldn't be likely to sail for a while yet. So I put on a heavy overcoat, went uptown, and caught a streetcar for Duluth.

I had been in the movie house for an hour when I began to feel a nagging uneasiness. The boat might sail. Finally, my apprehension hurried me out of the theater and onto the first streetcar back to Allouez. It didn't alleviate my fears that the bridge over the St. Louis River was opened to let a vessel through on her way downlakes. Finally, the bridge closed, the streetcar proceeded, and I alighted. I heard the hoarse whistle of a freighter leaving the ore dock. I picked up the skirts of my coat and ran the three blocks downhill to the dock, only to see the *King* out in the harbor, casting off her tug and turning for the breakwater opening.

My heart was in my mouth as I ran out on the dock. I had a vision of myself stranded in Duluth that winter. I had fifty cents in my pocket and the clothes on my back.

Climbing the flight of steps to the outer mooring walk of the ore dock, I saw the tug on its way back to its station. As it came abreast of me, I hailed, "Ahoy, Captain, will you take me out to the *King*?"

Great was my relief when the tug turned toward me and hosed in within a foot or two of the dock. I jumped the narrow space and clung to her stem post, standing on the rub strake outside her low rail. She turned then and, pushing through the broken ice of the harbor, headed for the freighter. Approaching the ship, the ice piling up against the steamer's flank only permitted the tug to come within about six feet. I made a leap, grabbed the steamer's wire rail with both hands, and pulled myself aboard.

Turning then, with a wave of my arm, I called to the tug's skipper, "Thanks a lot, Cap." I never knew whether the tug company made a charge for the service.

When, on my way forward, I saw Captain Reid of the *King*, I was not in the least disturbed by his gruff query, "Where in hell have *you* been?" I was that glad to get back.

Editor's note: On another leave, Fred Dutton had occasion to guide ship guests on the Schoonmaker *ashore at Duluth. He took them to Skyline Drive at dawn and startled himself.*

The driver headed the cab up the precipitous streets until, in the half-dawn, he pulled up at the base of the memorial tower high on the rocky heights above the city. Leaving the cab behind, the two ladies and the other two men and I scrambled up the path and then climbed to the top of the tower while a cold north wind whipped us. When we stepped out on the platform, I suppressed a gasp of amazement at the sheer glory spread out before us. Below, Duluth and the immense harbor lay silent, sleeping, shrouded in the mists, while out beyond over the vast expanse of Lake Superior to the east, as though a great curtain had been drawn revealing some celestial stage, the sun, not yet showing over the horizon, sent its fiery torch across the sky. I thought to myself that never before had I seen the magnificent lake so sublimely lit. It always held something new in store, if only one took the least trouble to look for it. Most mortals, it occurred to me, never felt the urge to rise in the morning early enough to see a sunrise. It was a moment that lifted one's spirit to dizzy heights—a moment to be engraved on the memory forever.

Our little party descended speechlessly to the earth and silently reentered the cab.

We found the ship nearly loaded, and soon the lines were cast off. She headed out through the two bridges spanning the St. Louis River and down the harbor for the open lake.

LOGS

"Warning to all mariners! Warning to all mariners!" The ship-to-shore burst into life. "Coast Guard bulletin, July 18, six P.M. All mariners are notified to be on the lookout for a

Hauling a forest to carry next month's news.

boom of logs on Lake Superior in the vicinity of Devil's Island. The boom of logs, in tow of the tug *Mary K*, left Grand Marais about six P.M. July 16 and is expected to cross the steamer lanes around eight P.M. July 18. Mariners are warned to keep a sharp lookout."

The second mate and I looked ahead then but saw nothing. We were still a couple of dozen miles from Devil's Island.

"Sure be a pretty mess if we hit one of those log booms," the mate commented. "Could do a lot of damage to the ship, and there'd be logs all over the lake for three months."

Half an hour later, I saw a small tug heading across our course four or five miles off starboard bow. I called it to the mate's attention; he got the binoculars and watched it for a time.

"That's him, all right. And his bearing doesn't change, either." He got the bearing finder and placed it against the window and swung the vanes to bring the tug into the slits. "No sir, she keeps her same bearing. Let her go left about ten degrees. That ought to clear her."

I put the wheel up a half a turn, and the ship swung slowly to port, then I steadied her. The second mate continued to take bearings on the tug from time to time, and finally it was apparent that the tug would be passed safely to starboard. The tug wasn't more than ninety feet in length, I saw when I had put the freighter back on her original course. The boom of logs strung out astern of the tug for half a mile—perhaps a quarter of a million logs—pulpwood for the Wisconsin paper mills, floating free in an encircling loop chained together end to end. It was like a huge lasso. So long as the lake remained fairly calm, the logs remained inside the boom. But should a storm come up, the seas would lift the restraining ring of chained logs, and the free logs within would escape. If the storm were severe enough, almost the entire boom would be lost. The run across the lake takes two or three days, and storms can arise quickly. There are always pulpwood logs floating around all over Lake Superior. Floating singly, these logs are not large enough to do any damage to a freighter. You'll feel a slight thump under the bow, but you think nothing of it. The logs drift about, here and there, and finally are washed up on the beach on the American or Canadian side of the lake, firewood for thousands of campers and natives over the entire two thousand miles of Lake Superior shoreline.

CHANGING THE WATCH

The change of watch at night is a thing you find yourself remembering. When you see how tame it is, you'll wonder why. But I figured it out one night.

I swallowed the last of my coffee, grabbed an orange and a handful of gingersnaps, and left the galley to go on watch. It was ten minutes before midnight, a gorgeous, bright night with a chrome-white moon laying on Lake Huron a track of light that shimmered and sparkled from the horizon right up to the ship. There was no sound but the soft whisper of warm wind off the Michigan shore and the chuckling of small waves along the steamer's flanks. I drank the heady wind as I climbed to the wheelhouse. I paused then for a moment to feel the intoxication of the night.

There's an unwritten law among seamen on the lakes. You relieve the watch a few minutes ahead of the hour. You are never late if you can possibly help it. You know full well how the minutes drag at the end of the watch before your relief comes. It always comes as just a little bit of a pleasant surprise when he walks in a couple minutes early with a "Good morning, gentlemen" or some original insult. So you always try to reciprocate and pass the courtesy along to the third fellow who has the four-hour watch between your relief and you.

So I paused in my reverie only a moment, then climbed the last steps to the pilothouse and opened the door. "Greetings to you, merry sailor men!" The second mate was just coming on watch with me. I moved over beside Jack, the wheelsman, lit a cigarette. "OK, Jack, I'll take her."

"All right, if you say so. Of course, I hate to let her go. After all, she really takes an expert, you know."

"True. That's why I never could understand why they trust guys like you with a five-million-dollar steamboat."

Jack released the wheel. "She's going 341."

"OK. Going 341."

"Good night." Jack went out into the night.

Another watch began. The familiar routine—the comfortable familiarity of it all. The third mate snapped out the light over the chart table as he and the second mate went over the situation. "There's Thunder Bay Island Light, Bob. Just got a four-point bearing. About five miles off. You can see the buoy ahead there. We ought to be abreast of it in ten minutes. Wind's southwest—about ten miles. I've got her steering 341 degrees. Old Man turned in an hour ago. Wants to be called half an hour before we pass Detour Light. We ought to be there about six o'clock."

The two mates indulged in a few minutes of insults. The third mate said, "Good night," and was gone.

The minutes passed. We left the buoy to port as the second mate took a bearing on Middle Island Light. Half an hour later, he stood by the bearing finder as the steamer brought the lighthouse abreast, its brilliant green flash rivaled by the moonlight on the water. He stood leaning over in an odd position, his hands on the windowsill, squinting through the vanes.

"How is she now, Fred?"

"She's right on 341." I had been steadying the ship down to a fine hair during the past two or three minutes.

"OK. I got her. You can steer 325." And he snapped on the light over the clock on the wall, noting the time, while I brought the ship around to the new course.

"Yep, just about seven miles off—thirty-four and a half minutes." He did some figuring on a pad.

It was a dandy night. The second mate and I were feeling good. The breeze whimpered sadly in the rigging. The roaring of the water under the ship's stern was muted and forgotten. We were too accustomed to it to notice.

The wheelhouse talk flowed. Middle Island's green flash was left astern, and Presque Isle loomed abeam. The blink of Detour Reef's gleaming eye showed from beyond the horizon, fifty miles away, like heat lightning on a summer evening. At four bells, the watchman brought the coffee kit and poured all around. I surrendered the wheel to Hank, who perched himself on the stool with his coffee cup sitting in front of him on the standard compass binnacle. I sat back in luxury in the captain's high chair. This was life!

I wondered why, when I thought of other ships, the change of the night watch was what I most remembered. Then it came to me: the smoothness of the change of watch, when the captain is asleep, is how you judge the quality of a ship . . . or any organization.

SKIPPERS AND SUCH

Most of the captains and mates on the lake vessels were ordinarily quiet-voiced men, and often I had difficulty hearing the skipper's orders given while steering in the rivers. This was of extreme importance, and on occasion it worried me and made me nervous, for a very small mistake in a narrow river can bend up a lot of plate steel.

Captain Scaffer on the *Horace Johnson* spoke in a particularly low voice when directing the wheelsman—and it didn't help that he was usually leaning out the pilothouse window, so that I often couldn't tell whether the skipper was speaking to me or the watchman or the mate. Most of the time, there was a running conversation between the skipper and the mate, lost in which now and again was an order to "Right some" or "A little faster left," or "Steady her there." Consequently, I found it necessary to strain my ears constantly to try and catch the scrap of an order. But even so, I sometimes missed, and on such occasions the mate usually would turn and look at me, and perhaps gesture with his hand indicating the turn to right or left. But occasionally I had to speak up and say, "What was that, sir?" or "Did you say right?" It was embarrassing sometimes.

Of course, I knew the rivers well enough that for the

131

most part I knew where to turn and was in a position to anticipate the order; but no two skippers run the rivers exactly the same way. Each has his own way of approaching and making a turn—sometimes the skipper and the mate will even get into an argument about it. However, captains tend to violate Robert's Rules of Debate and overstay the allotted rebuttal time. And then, when the captain has gone below, the mate pours out his grievance on the subject. Captain Scaffer had a peculiar habit in giving an order to the wheelsman of saying "Slow" as though he had said "Oh"; and sometimes when the skipper said "Oh," I would take a chance that he had said "Slow," and would take the helm off her to slow down her swing. But this sometimes got me into trouble, and the skipper would turn and rather acidly order, "Keep her coming there, don't take the wheel off of her yet!" It was often a relief to me when the skipper went below, and then I in turn would pour out my troubles about the skipper to the mate.

On one occasion, I was steering the steamship up the St. Clair River on a particularly black night, and the captain, leaning on the windowsill as usual, told me, "Now, if you find that I am standing here so you can't see the light on the steering pole, you just tell me about it and I'll move."

So I told him on two or three occasions that I couldn't see, and the captain cheerfully moved over. But finally, I sensed that the captain was becoming irritated about it; so after that when the skipper stood right in the middle of the front window, shutting off my view, I just stood up on my tiptoes so I could look over his head. It was a little awkward and something of a strain, but it sufficed, and when I got tired standing on my toes that way, I'd either steer a compass course or else stand a little to one side, roughly estimating a course a few inches to the right or left of the steering pole.

A captain's speech habit can be a navigation hazard. There was a Captain Macklin, a Scot with a thick burr. It seems he was running the rivers one night, and he gave an order to his wheelsman. The wheelsman was a bit green, not accustomed to Captain Macklin's manner of speech, and he walked away from the wheel and started for the door. The captain looked around and made a grab for the wheel, calling the wheelsman back: "Where in the devil d'y'think yer goin', mon? You should no take yer hands off the wheel!" The wheelsman looked sheepish as he took the wheel again. The captain repeated the order: "Let her come faster." The wheelsman replied, "Oh, I thought you said 'Get the hell out of here!' "

The captain on the *Schoonmaker* was as at home and easy on the water as a walrus on a rock.

There was a full-sized summer northeastern blasting Lake Huron one night as the *Schoonmaker* thrashed up the lake off Thunder Bay. The course was changed to 360 degrees on the gyro, which soon caused the freighter to roll violently. The mate ordered me to let her go 020, and when she eased off her rolling a bit, he ordered her back to 360. And then she rolled way down to port again, a door banged down below, and dishes crashed in the passenger quarters. The great 590-foot steamer, upbound light, pushed her forward end out of the water and came down on the next sea with a boom that felt like solid rock. A moment later, Captain Deahl burst through the doorway to the pilothouse, cheerfully remarking, "This is some damn breeze. Better put some more water in her, Joe."

"Well, sir," the mate replied, "she's got about twelve feet

in numbers 4, 5, and 6"—taking a quick look at the small
blackboard hanging on the back wall—"and she's got three
to six feet in 1, 2, and 3."

"Guess you better run some more in forward, Joe," said
the skipper. "And let's put some in the forepeak, eh?"

The mate picked the phone off the wall and cranked the
engine room. "John, open up 1, 2, and 3. And run some
water in the forepeak, will you?"

He turned to the deck watch. "Roy, get down there in
half an hour and sound those tanks again. I want six feet in
1 and 2 and about eight in 3."

The skipper perched comfortably on his high chair
when the *Schoonmaker* threw herself into another violent
roll to port, spilling the skipper onto the floor and tipping me off my stool. I saved myself only by hanging on
to the wheel, whereupon I decided it was time to stand
up to do the steering. The captain chuckled as he picked
himself up and stood the chair upright. "About time to
head her into it, Joe. We'll be smashing things up down
below."

The mate told me to bring her around to about twenty-
five degrees. I spun the wheel over a turn and watched the
gyro as it started to click over. Quickly I had her steadied on
the new course; the rolling subsided, though the ship continued pitching. But soon the added ballast in her water
bottom steadied her so that she wasn't out of the water
anymore. When I was relieved at eight bells, the seas were
gradually lessening as the ship began to feel the lee of
Manitoulin Island on the Canadian side.

Through it all, if you'd glance at Deahl's face, it was
bemused tolerance—like if he really had to shut off the
storm, he could.

That's one type of captain.

134

It was a continual source of interest and amusement to me to listen to the jargon spoken by many of the sailors on the freighters. When a young fellow ships out as a deckhand, he hears this sailor talk on every side. Few sailors seem to be able to say more than three or four words without some raunchy oath, obviously a mark of manhood.

However, the majority of the lake sailors seem to outgrow profanity when they become captains. Some skippers never use it at all, others only in minor emergencies. Few of them use profanity in serious emergencies. Some of them are of a nervous temperament and fly off the handle now and then. A few appear to be under a continual state of nervous collapse—high-strung, excitable, they curse by second nature. The responsibility of the captain's work and the loneliness often tend to make him introspective and irritable.

Frankly, a captain is not likely to be a great conversationalist, almost by definition. He is apt to know everything about the ship and its envelope of water and weather. But being captive on a six hundred-foot moving island for most of his working life, his conversation often concerns a six hundred-foot world.

The lakes officers usually have little in their makeup suggestive of the traditional bucko mate or iron-fisted skipper, as in the early days. Most are intelligent, amiable, considerable officers with whom it is a pleasure to work.

The personnel of many lake vessels are like a happy family, with no perceptible distinction in rank between the mates and the men, although there is ordinarily not much fraternization between the men and the captain. The skipper is not by choice an autocrat, but by the nature of his position he is apart from the crew and leads a somewhat lonely existence.

The steel jungle, home of the steamers. (Alan W. Sweigert photo.)

He often takes part in the sailor talk in the pilothouse, but there is a noticeable restraint when he is present. I often noticed that when the skipper enters the pilothouse, the conversation immediately ceases its easy flow. There may be stories, banter, the recounting of experiences, gossip concerning captains of other ships, about vessel owners and managers, intimate gossip about women (a subject that occupies at least half the sailors' time), but it isn't the same. The mate and the wheelsman may be carrying on a lively conversation about anything under the sun, but the instant the skipper appears the talk stops. Any further conversation is on a different plane. The Old Man is the Old Man!

No one resents it. But there is a barrier that cannot be brushed aside. There is a tacit understanding that the Old Man carries a big load, not to be underestimated.

The captain rarely displays his authority overtly. Usually his orders are stated quietly in the form of a request or a sort of tentative suggestion. But it is law. His responsibility is great, and he is a man of almost superhuman competence and decision. He cannot afford to make a mistake. He makes a suggestion mildly to the mate, and the mate carries it out promptly, efficiently, thoroughly. It is a good system.

I've sailed with captains who were as calm and cool as ice. And I have worked under others who raged and swore.

Captain Danison on the *Sinoloa* was the volcanic profanity type, swearing for any reason, or no reason, yet his crew was fond of him. He was bringing the *Sinoloa* into the Republic dock on the Cuyahoga River in Cleveland one morning in fine style. He loved to come up to the dock smartly, then stop her with the engines suddenly reversed and the rudder hard over. But this time, when he rang for full astern, the engines didn't respond, and the *Sinoloa*'s stern hammered into the concrete dock, cracking her starboard hawse pipe and relieving the dock of a large hunk of concrete. It was a fine sight to see and hear the skipper jumping up and down out there on the bridge, fulminating at the mate as he ordered him to get down there and throw some water on the break in the concrete so it wouldn't look so new. I leaned on the wheel and swallowed a grin.

Captain Shores of the *Little Chief* was a chronic nervous wreck, fearing disaster at every turn. Though he didn't often raise his voice or break out into profanity, a crisis unfailingly threw him into a tizzy, and the resulting fireworks were a sight to remember. The *Little Chief* was a barge, one of the largest on the lakes, with a capacity of 210,000 bushels of grain. She carried a crew of sixteen as she was being towed by the steamer *Western Star* in the grain trade from Fort William to Buffalo. A fresh north wind was pushing the *Little Chief* sidewards as the two vessels came around on the Bayfield Range and headed for the locks at the Soo. Captain Shores wanted to stop at the fuel dock for bunker coal, but the skipper of the steamer got the signals mixed up, and, instead of pulling the barge alongside, he dropped the towline and left the barge charging helplessly toward the coal dock. With a scream, Captain Shores blew his stack, and, raging back and forth on the bridge, he ordered the mates to drop the anchors, he howled to the wheelsman to put her hard right, he cursed and bewailed, but the barge plowed on into the dock and bounced off, cracking a couple of plates and parting a mooring cable. I looked for the skipper to drop dead of apoplexy.

I decided I should learn more first aid.

A pair of young lady passengers were aboard one trip on the old *St. Clair*. It was a fine bright morning as the freighter slid silently along up the Detroit River past Fighting Island. The two young women were up in the wheelhouse enjoying the scenery in the river, when one of them commented to Captain Trimble on the fact that he never used profanity; it didn't seem in keeping with all they had heard about sailors. The captain, who was never anything but courtly, and who spoke with a slight stutter, looked upriver for a while, then asked mildly, "W-w-would you l-l-like to hear a s-s-sailor s-s-swear?"

The young lady was a little taken aback, but having gone that far, she cast discretion to the winds and said that perhaps it would seem more in character—just a little, maybe.

Half an hour later, the *St. Clair* had overhauled and was passing a small wooden lumber hooker, and as the two ships came abreast, Captain Trimble stepped out on the bridge wing and called through the megaphone: "It's a w-w-wonder you w-w-wouldn't g-g-get your d-d-dirty old s-s-scow out of the w-w-way!"

To which the skipper of the lumber hooker, who knew Captain Trimble well, let loose a torrent of sulfurous seagoing abuse which rolled sonorously across the water and echoed back from the far shore. The two young ladies turned crimson and fled the pilothouse.

Captain Trimble was also a man of great delicacy, which required considerable ingenuity. For example, two days later, the captain discovered the two ladies again in the wheelhouse, one of them standing rather close to the binnacle. The wheelsman mentioned to the captain that the compass was acting in a very odd way. Captain Trimble studied the two girls, then spoke gently to the one who had red hair. "Perhaps you'd best not stand so close to the compass. Red hair attracts the needle."

The young lady moved away in some confusion, and the needle straightened up. She probably later amazed many people with this information about redheads. She never learned from the captain that it was the steel stays in her corset that affected the compass. Changing fashions first eliminated this difficulty on steamships, then the gyro compass did away with dependence on magnetic forces.

Captains come in very interesting styles.

On another occasion, I was taking the *John T. Hutchinson* into Two Harbors. She was a brand new vessel, 620 feet in length, with a capacity of some 14,850 tons of iron ore, and her pilothouse was something like 60 feet above the water. She was light, of course, and most of her ballast water had been pumped out. The fine new steamship nosed slowly up to the ore dock, on an angle, for the dock was on the port side, and when the engines were reversed it would throw the ship's stern to port and bring her neatly alongside the dock.

The cool and able Captain Jacobsen was given charge of this new beauty. He pushed the handle of the Chadburn down to full speed astern and looked aft out the windows to watch her swing. I automatically glanced at the engine indicator on the wall over the front window. Nothing happened. The engines had stuck on dead center, and before they could be started astern, the great vessel struck the dock, catching her fo'c'sle and bridge deck railings and bulwarks on the lower ends of the ore dock spouts. There was a great crashing and screaming of rending steelwork. A pained look spread over Captain Jacobsen's face as he turned to me, but all he said was, "Well, there go the railings."

It must have hurt him deeply to have his fine, new steamship messed up so. But he was not a screamer.

However, I did hear him cuss once. The *Hutchinson* was proceeding down through the narrow channel of Hay Lake, eight or nine miles below the Soo. It was a dark night, with a bit of fog. The visibility was about two or three miles. A dim light appeared out of the murk dead ahead a half a mile. Captain Jacobsen blew a blast on the whistle. Getting no answer, he blew another. As there was no answer the second time, he blew a danger signal—several short blasts—and rang for full speed astern, ordering the wheel hard left to counteract the steamer's swing as the propeller took hold, and almost in the same breath he told the third mate, "Go below and drop the anchor."

The third mate didn't touch the treads on the companionways. Hands on the rails, he slid down three flights and tore into the windlass room. The chain cable rattled, and the starboard anchor plunged to the bottom, caught mud, and dragged.

It isn't easy to stop an 8,000-ton steamship loaded with 16,000 tons of iron ore downbound in the St. Marys River where the current flows at two or three miles per hour.

But finally, agonizingly, the great steamer stopped—a bare fifty feet from a large steel pulpwood barge which was lying square across the channel.

As the barge's tug dragged it around and out of the way, Captain Jacobsen leaned out of the window and politely inquired of the tug's skipper: "*Captain! Just what in the hell are you trying to do?*"

It was the only time I ever heard Captain Jacobsen roar.

Your captains and mates are important to you on a steamboat, but more important in one sense are your shipmates. I look back on some memorable ones.

Few realize how far into the twentieth century some schooners still worked. They were gone by the time Dutton went steamboating, but there were still officers in steamboat pilothouses whose first papers were for canvas. This is *Our Son* out of Milwaukee.

Hank Kilfoyle was the watchman in our watch, a fine sailor and a competent seaman. He could tell stories by the hour about his experiences all over the world—in jail and out—in a manner that held you spellbound. The night watches in the wheelhouse with him and the coffee sessions afterwards in the galley were something to anticipate. To have such a man in a crew is a lucky thing. Kilfoyle's stories were always told with the skill of a master painter, and they were educational, even subtracting 20 percent for fiction.

Hank had even done a stretch in Alcatraz for enlisting in the army under an assumed name.

He was skilled in many other ways. He could make almost anything out of an old orange crate with a jackknife.

Sailors are of necessity about the most resourceful fellows in the world anywhere. They have to be able to make things out of practically nothing, with the simplest tools. An A.B. worth his salt can do almost anything. He is a sailor first, but he is an all-around plumber and electrician and a pretty good carpenter or even a cabinetmaker. He can splice, weave, sew, darn, and do macramé. There's hardly anything you might ask him to do that he can't do. And he usually never tries to do anything unless he does it well. But Kilfoyle was way above average.

Especially, he was a real sailor. He was also mighty accomplished when it came to drinking. And as he never did things by halves, every time he got into port, he came back to the ship tighter than a boiled owl. He would sleep through a couple of watches. And so, the first twenty-four hours after the ship left port, somebody had to stand his watch a couple of times for him. And that was all right; everybody understood about it. He never missed the boat; they all knew that, too, and they appreciated it.

But the big thing about Kilfoyle was—except for what I have just explained—you could always count on his great seamanship to put the good of the ship first. The ship is a sailor's nation. If on shore we could count on shoremates as devoted as most shipmates, it would be a beautiful country.

CHAPTER IX

WEATHER!

Editor's Note: Weather is half a sailor's professional life. He answers to mates and captains, of course, but the ultimate boss is still Dame Nature. Fred Dutton danced a few storms with her at different times in his life.

LAST OF THE *MAGGIE*

It looked pretty black in the north, with low clouds driving along on a strong wind that moaned in the rigging, rising now and then in a climbing banshee crescendo that shivered my spine.

That was when I was a youngster wheeling on the old *Maggie*. She was already an old wooden tub, long past prime, carrying ore during the World War I shortage of bottoms.

Downbound, we were passing Detour Reef Light. Lake Huron's expanse, stretching ahead, had a forbidding look. The land on either side of the passage lay dim and ghostlike astern, the more so while the green flash of Frying Pan blinked back there in the darkening.

Heavily laden, her deck but a few feet above the water, the barge *Maggie*, converted from one of the last of the old wooden schooners, rolled a little on the rising swells as she wallowed along on her towline behind the steamer *Emberly*.

I felt a little lonely on my watch at the wheel in *Maggie*'s tiny square box of a wheelhouse. I sat there on my stool, keeping my eyes glued on the *Emberly*'s white range light, giving the wheel a spoke now and then to keep the old barge just a little left of the steamer's wake. You can't steer a barge directly behind her steamer; she'll yaw back and forth across the wake all the time.

The hours dragged. Six hours at the wheel is a long time alone in a wheelhouse.

Finally, toward the end of the watch, the mate opened the lee door, which nearly knocked him off his feet as it flew open in the wind suction on that side. He couldn't have opened the weather-side door. The wind across open lake nailed it shut.

"Damn dirty night." He shivered some in the little pilothouse. "Don't like this much. Might get into Thunder Bay."

As he spoke, the barge slid sideways and gave a dead sort of lurch as a good-sized sea mounted the rail and buried the amidships deck.

"Don't like it either," my relief wheelsman commented. He turned and glanced out the after window and looked forward again as the old barge fought free of the seas. "Hatches won't stand much more of that," he continued.

The door burst open, and the watchman backed in, bracing both feet against the sill to pull the door shut.

"How much water has she got in her?" asked the mate.

"Two feet in Number 1 and four feet aft," reported the watchman. "A lot of water. The old girl is opening up."

"Hell, yes," replied the mate. "Rouse the Old Man."

The watchman left, and pretty soon the captain appeared, the wind a full-throated roar when the door was thrown back, screaming up the scale again and sticking on a high note as the Old Man pulled the door behind him.

"She's got four feet of water in her, sir," the mate shouted above the gale. "We've just passed Presque Isle."

Seas were coming over the deck more frequently. A white shape reared out of the darkness to windward, swept across the deck, and with a ripping explosion collided with the pilothouse. The men ducked as the windows burst inward, spraying glass. The sea flooded the wheelhouse.

The wheelsman was scared but held on, standing in water that sloshed around his knees as the barge rolled. Captain Warner opened the lee door to let the water out. The wheelsman couldn't see to steer for the spray coming in the broken windows. He was all but blind.

"We can't make it." The captain reached for the whistle cord and pulled eight or ten times. We waited. There was no answer from the *Emberly*, but the barge wallowed on.

"Are all the men aft?" inquired the captain, shouting to make himself heard. He motioned to the watchman to go and find out. "God, I hope they hear us." And he jerked the whistle cord again, sending out nine long blasts and one short squeak; the boiler wasn't built for such continuous blowing.

The crew was gathering at the single lifeboat, starboard, tying on life belts. The mate reached up and yanked the cord that held the life belts to the ceiling. He handed them to the captain and the wheelsman. "Put this on! I'll hold her." And he took the wheel.

"Hell of a night to swim in Lake Huron," complained

Some sights reminded passing crews to write home. Some ten thousand ships lie on the bottom of the Great Lakes. (W. A. McDonald photo.)

Captain Warner with—I couldn't believe it—a smile. Then they heard a faint, faraway whistle from the steamer, answering their distress call.

"She's losing way," cried the mate. "He's coming about!"

The *Emberly's* lights showed she was turning into the wind. Around she came, slowly, making a full circle. As she turned, they heard, louder now that she was to windward, the steamer's signal that she was dropping the towline.

Captain Warner blew the answering signal. "Well," he remarked, "the towline's on the bottom now; that'll hold us a bit. No man could get forward in this sea."

They watched while the steamer came abreast, a hundred feet off port side. She lay there then, rolling heavily, but in her lee the seas were noticeably less.

"Get that boat over," ordered the skipper. "Come on, all of you, into the boat." He followed us out the door. The barge's deck was awash. The crew—twelve men—tumbled into the lifeboat, followed by the captain.

"Lower away," he yelled over the wind. They didn't have far to lower; the barge was going down under them.

"Cast off," yelled the captain as the boat struck the wa-

147

ter. "Out oars, and give way—smartly now! Your backs into it! Don't get us caught in her suction!"

Six men strained at the oars, and the boat moved away.

The old *Maggie* slid under. She was gone—swallowed.

Just a few floating hatch covers tossed in the glare from the *Emberly*'s searchlight sweeping the sea.

We pulled the short distance over to the steamer and under her lee. Lines came down; a ladder was put over. The crew of the *Maggie* climbed to the steamer's deck. They went aft to the galley for hot coffee, as the two captains congratulated each other and made their way forward.

When it was time to turn in, we doubled up with the *Emberly*'s crew, each man occupying another's berth while the owner was on watch.

Maggie was the last of the wooden barges.

When the ship arrived at Cleveland thirty-six hours later, the men had almost forgotten the old *Maggie* ever existed. After being paid off by the owners and filing a claim for possessions lost, they went home for a few days' rest before shipping out on another vessel.

But for me, the *Maggie* may have been my most important berth. It taught me, forever after, that man's big institutions, which may feel and look solid under your feet, are not. When they go down, they go fast. Ships, banks, industries. I remained always ready.

NOVEMBER BLOW: THE LONGEST TRIP

It *seemed* routine.

Captain Morrison opened the door to the pilothouse, strode over to the Chadburn, rang for standby, and pulled hard down on the whistle lever for the deck crew to cast off. Out on the bridge wing then, he watched as the deckhands on the dock lifted the wire cables from the bollards and let them fall in the water to be winched in. As the deckhands climbed over the wire rail onto the deck, he rang up the Chadburn to half astern and blew a long blast warning other vessels that *Cetus* was leaving the ore dock. We had taken a load of coal from Huron to Manitowoc, running light from there to Ashland, Wisconsin, for iron ore.

It was a biting cold November. The harbor at Ashland was a bleak gray, ruffled by whitecaps under a freshening northeaster driving down across Lake Superior. *Cetus* backed slowly around, an angry chop slapping her quarter, throwing a freezing spray onto the deck and after house. Now and again, snow flurries obscured my vision as I swung the loaded ship around for the harbor entrance.

Captain Morrison, like all lake skippers in the 'twenties, had to be his own weather forecaster. There was no radio, no ship-to-shore phone, no Lafot, no Laweb. All he had was the barometer, the clouds, direction and force of the wind . . . and experience.

Cetus had an upper or flying pilothouse and a lower wheelhouse. It was in the lower that I stood alone. The skipper called his occasional commands to the wheelsman down through the guff box over my head, for the skipper and the mates always navigated from the flying pilothouse. It was sometimes eerie to hear the voice of God calling down to me from above.

I straightened the steamer out as she came ahead, taking her outside the breakwater, and setting the course to the northeast along the length of Madeline Island, then Michigan Island.

After a while, she began to feel the full force of the northeaster, the ugly black seas rearing out of the dusk ahead, driven by the gale blowing across two hundred miles of open lake.

As night came on and the watch wore slowly along, the wind increased, the seas growing larger with the passing hours, reaching a height from trough to crest of thirty feet or more. *Cetus* buried her fo'c'sle head regularly, taking the enormous waves green over the bow, so that a good part of the time her lower pilothouse was under water. The portholes in the lower pilothouse were far from watertight, and with each sea coming over the bow, water spurted in around the portholes, flooding the floor six inches to the top of the doorsills. Adding to the misery of the next two or three watches were the loneliness and confinement of the small room and the endless roar of the gale and the crash of seas against the steel shell, a wet Dante's Inferno.

I sat on the stool, bracing myself on the wheel, for the most part keeping my feet out of the water. As for steering, the best I could do was to hold her within three or four points, for she showed an insane determination to yaw to one side, then the other. Frequently the magnetic compass (she had no gyro), rocking wildly in its gimbals, would go into circular gyrations, sometimes 360 degrees. At times, I had no slightest idea which direction she was heading, except for the direction of the waves. The basic principle was to keep her headed directly into the storm.

Since the temperature was near zero, the ship was accumulating a heavy coat of ice, adding dangerously to her weight and putting her deeper in the water. That made her even more difficult to steer.

None of us in the forward end got anything to eat through that night and the next. The seas flooding the deck made it impossible to get aft to the dining room. The ice alone would have made it extremely hazardous to venture aft. The deck was a skating rink. The after-end crew were having a wet time of it as well. The chief engineer reported over the phone that the galley was flooded out three or four times, while all the rooms aft had a good deal of water slopping about on the floor. In the engine room, bilge water sloshed over the floor plates, and an occasional shower came from the skylight. Everyone on the ship was miserable.

The icing of the vessel had one beneficial result: it sealed the portholes. Water only got in around the doors.

As the watches dragged on, Captain Morrison appeared calm, but his voice showed some strain. The vessel labored and rolled, pitched and bounced, and sprung up and down amidships. But she was making some headway against the gale. Sometimes she would fall off almost into the trough, rolling horribly, first one rail under and then the other. The danger was that she might shift her cargo; then the next sea might roll her right over.

The snow, which increased the second night, was a worry. The course we were steering, roughly northeast by east, if we could assume she was approximating that, would bring us safely past Passage Island and off the Slate Islands in some thirty-six hours or more. But the snow obscured everything, and the captain and the mates were by no means certain just where we were. The hours dragged. Captain, mate, and watchman strained their eyes into the driving snow, but no one could see anything besides the seas and the snow. Nor could they hear any sound but the storm.

I came off watch at midnight after another six hours at the wheel. Although I was exhausted from trying to keep the laboring vessel on her course, sleep would not come. The wild rolling slid me back and forth from the head of my bunk to the foot. No amount of bracing helped. Also, the seas slamming against the bows, lifting and dropping the anchors in their hawse pipes, banged sleep out of the question. I dressed and went up to the wheelhouse to keep my partner wheelsman company, occupying myself with bailing out the water when the seas permitted. Opening the door between waves to toss out a bucket of water required some timing. Often more water came in than went out.

Toward dawn, I heard a sudden shout from the mate in the flying pilothouse. During a lull in the snowstorm, he had caught a glimpse of land off the port bow and had seen a flash of a light. A relieved babble was heard from the three men up there.

It was Slate Island—right where it ought to be.

Only luck had made good the course we had been trying to steer for thirty-six hours. You could hardly call it good steering.

The seas were diminishing noticeably as we approached the north shore of the lake. Soon Captain Morrison called down through the guff box, "Let her go sou'east by south." The lake here, under the lee of the shore, was almost calm by comparison. We steered *Cetus* along the lee shore, passing between Michipicoten Island and the north shore to Whitefish Bay and the Soo.

She was a sight going through the locks, coated from bow to stern with several hundred tons of ice, huge icicles trailing from the forward railings. She was leaking, having lost several hundred rivets through the springing of her hull.

It was the longest trip I had ever made down the lake, 60 hours from Ashland to the Soo. But beyond that, I think it is the longest trip I ever steered in my life.

HOLED AND STRANDED

Sailors are always tense when fog sets in.

The *Hosford* had only the barest headway. Parisienne Island was well astern, and she slowly drifted down past

152

Gros Cap lightship and Point Iroquois. It was night, and a pea-soup fog had shut down about an hour before. Whistles sounded mournful on all sides—three blasts each minute. A large freighter lay at anchor a bit to starboard, another just ahead.

Captain Jacobsen couldn't see a thing.

On the fo'c'sle head, the watchman peered out, straining his eyes into the dripping fog; turning now and again, he reported a whistle or rapid ringing of a ship's bell. The whistles—in groups of three blasts—indicated a ship under way; the bells were vessels at anchor. It was getting too uncomfortable to keep going. Sailors hate fog.

An upbound steamer's shape loomed ghostly on the port bow.

"Right some, and give that fellow a little more room," Captain Jacobsen ordered quietly. I put the wheel down a turn.

I wasn't very happy. Correction: I was scared. These steamers were too close . . . and too many.

This place, where all courses on Lake Superior converged into the narrow channel above the Soo, was one of the worst places on the lakes in a fog. Vessels' bones lay thick on the bottom here in 150 feet of cold water. These waters made a lot of widows.

Captain Jacobsen rang the Chadburn to half astern, at the same time ordering me to put her amidships.

"I guess you better drop the hook, Joe." He spoke quietly to the first mate. Big, lanky, competent Joe left the pilot-house and ran down below to the windlass room. When the steamer lost headway, the skipper rang the engines to stop and called into the speaking tube, "OK, Joe."

The mate's voice came back faintly. The anchor chain shuddered in the hawse pipe like dumping a truckload of boulders, followed by an occasional knock as an extra link or two of chain ran out. Slowly the ship swung about with the current as the anchor took hold. With the cessation of all motion in the ship, the silence was earsplitting. Now and then came three blasts of a whistle and a bell rapidly rung. I added to the chorus, ringing the *Hosford*'s bell violently once a minute. As the steamer turned, I watched the gyro card giving off its soft *click, click, click*—six times for each degree the ship swung.

"Cripes, it's thick," mumbled the mate. "You could cut your initials in it." Nobody answered.

Captain Jacobsen's expression was always a kind of bemused sadness. More so now. "Well, I suppose we'll lie here for six hours, anyway, unless . . ."

A whistle sounded. Close.

"Steamer downbound, dead ahead!" came from the fo'c'sle watch. The wheelhouse went silent. Senses sharpened. I grabbed the bell pull and shattered the stillness. The first mate swore.

Swinging from side to side in the current, the *Hosford*'s heading changed, but the only audible sounds were the slow *click, click* of the gyro, and now and then a slight thump below as the anchor chain shifted. The fog presented a blind wall at the pilothouse windows, enclosing us claustrophobically. Wisps of the clammy white misted in through the open front window.

Again the stranger's whistle blast broke in—one, two, three times—on the starboard this time, for the *Hosford* had swung at anchor. Captain Jacobsen put the phone to his ear and dialed.

"*Hosford* calling the steamer downbound below Iroquois! *Hosford* calling the downbound steamer!"

A wild yell from the lookout shattered the night. "Steamer four points on starboard bow! Steamer . . ."

Captain Jacobsen dropped the phone on its hook. He

stared off the quarter as the mate sprang out the door onto the bridge. Rooted, I watched a great black ship coming toward us with deadly, irresistible momentum.

A terrible cry from the other ship, then the crash. Steel tortured steel. We regained our footing. But the *Hosford* shook violently as the other vessel scraped along, then slowly drew away.

We had a deep gash, starboard, at the second hatch.

The skipper threw the switch. The alarm bells rang throughout the ship. The first mate pulled the lever, sounding general alarm.

"Get back there, Joe." The captain's voice was urgent. "Get the collision mat over. Get mattresses, anything. See how much damage! Sound the tanks!"

Captain Jacobsen was out on the starboard bridge then, calling the other steamer through the megaphone: "Stand by, Captain, you may have to take off my crew."

But the other vessel was gone in the fog.

We could hear the roar of Lake Superior pouring into our hold.

"Captain, we can't do a thing!" shouted the mate from the spar deck. "She's going down! Nothing will hold the water!" The skipper blew "abandon ship" on the big whistle; men ran to the lifeboats. We hadn't been at our stations two minutes before the boats were swung out, ready to lower. I had never seen a crew work so fast.

But Captain Jacobsen made a sudden decision. He used the phone to the engineer: "Chief, I'm going to try to beach her. Give me everything you've got." Then he rang the Chadburn to full ahead. A moment later, he repeated it for more speed. The Chadburn rang its answer. The pointer swung to full speed ahead. Captain Jacobsen took the wheel and spun it hard over left. The *Hosford* was now very low in the water. Slowly, with agonizing deliberation, she gathered way.

In the windlass room, the second mate had the windlass heaving madly on the anchor to free it.

The captain megaphoned the after end of the ship, still invisible in the fog. "Hold the boats, Joe! I am going to beach her!"

"Aye, aye, Captain!"

With a quick look at the Upper St. Marys River chart, Jacobsen estimated the vessel's position and picked a spot on the shore of nearby Waiska Bay on the American side of the river. He knew there was a beach with sand bottom.

A steamer's bell was heard ahead, and Jacobsen put the wheel over. Lying there at anchor, another steamer slid past a bare arm's length off port side. Minutes passed. Lower and lower the vessel sank, the water halfway to her deck.

The men stood by the boats. Firemen and engine-room crew below worked like demons. Fortunately, the bulkhead was holding; the fire hold remained dry. The clang of shovels told us of the fireman's effort to keep up steam.

There was also the thump and wheeze of the big triple and the clattering pumps trying vainly to hold back the water, plus occasional whistles and yells.

The water now was within inches of the deck. The captain was silent, almost motionless, except to turn the wheel a spoke or two. His face showed nothing. It was as though he were steering the ship in open lake on a clear day.

Small waves began to lap over the gunwales onto the deck. On the after-cabin top, the men waited with tortured nerves for an order to abandon ship. Would the Old Man never give the order? Was he out of his mind?

Suddenly a tremor ran through the vessel; a giant hand shoved her back. The men were thrown forward, and some lost their balance.

The *Hosford* stopped, swung around a little, and rested there. A shout burst from the crew.

He had made it!

She was on the bottom and could sink no further. Captain Jacobsen called the Coast Guard on the ship-to-shore and sent a message to his owners.

For a couple of days, I had almost nothing to do while the wreckers patched the hole in the steamer's side and lightened her a bit and pumped her out, with the help of the Hosford's own pumps, so that she was soon floated again and ready for the five-mile run down the river to the Algoma Steel Company's dock at the Canadian Soo.

After she was unloaded, it was no great job to patch her up, because the hole in her side was well above waterline.

As the Hosford made her way down the rivers again a week later, Captain Jacobsen remarked with a wry smile concerning the Algoma layover, "I wouldn't have minded so much, but they fined me a hundred dollars for landing in a foreign port without a clearance."

CHAPTER X

✹

FLASHBACKS

Editor's Note: In a long career, the veteran helmsman has mastered nearly every challenge. Here he comes up against one in the Detroit River which a lifetime's navigation skill won't help.

THE TYCOON

Once I was vacationing with my small son, Ted, at Marquette, visiting the scenes of my own childhood. As with all sailors, I was drawn to the waterfront, and we two—father and son—walked out on the ore dock. The dock was always a mysterious place—cool, deserted, silent. It was something like an immense cathedral with its high vaulted arches reaching up into dim space. The rows of tall concrete columns on either side stretched away in the distance, diminishing to the vanishing point; the dock was more than a quarter of a mile long.

I noticed as we walked along the plank walk in the middle of the dock that there was a large freighter tied up on the other side. She was one of Ford Motor's big ore carriers, the *Benson Ford*, a diesel. We mounted the short flight of steps and stood alongside the great ship, her side plating a high wall before us. Looking up, I spied a seaman at the rail—evidently one of the mates—and I called up, "Can we come aboard and look her over?"

After a hesitation, he answered, "Sorry. Guess you better not this time."

"What's going on?" I questioned. It was unusual to refuse a fellow seaman to come aboard.

"Well . . . I can't tell you. Sorry."

Curiosity aroused, we stood there for a little, wondering what was going to happen.

Sure enough, in a few minutes a shiny Ford pulled up at the shore end of the dock. Three passengers got out. There was sudden activity on the freighter. The gangplank thrust out from the engine-room gangway. And not an ordinary plank; it had railings, and the railings were wrapped with white cloth. Then a porter stepped out on the gangplank, rolling out a strip of red carpet.

"O-ho," I commented to my son. "Someone pretty big is boarding."

With a push broom, the porter swept the carpet and stationed himself at the plank.

Then I recognized the slim, slightly stooped man who stepped out on the dock with two ladies, a young one and an older one. Henry Ford himself. Not the chubby grand-son, mind you. I mean *Henry Ford*.

The two ladies went up the gangplank while Mr. Ford stopped and bought a copy of the *Marquette Mining Journal* from a newsboy who had joined us there on the dock. But Henry Ford passed up the gangplank. He made for the ladder hanging over the side of the great vessel that bore his grandson's name. Spry as a sailor, he swarmed up the ladder to the deck.

159

Benson Ford. (Alan W. Sweigert photo.)

As Ted and I turned toward the shore, the newsboy held up a coin. "Look, a quarter!"

It was the only time in my life that I saw the great automobile manufacturer, but I kept a deep and lasting impression of a simple, friendly man. If we ever would have had the chance to talk, I'll bet he would have liked to hear the story of the *Selkirk*. It was funny, but mostly it was grimly serious.

THE *SELKIRK*'S LOUD LOAD

The northwest gale was playing the rigging like an organ as I ran forward from the warm galley up to the wheelhouse. Captain Breed was standing by the whistle pull, looking aft. The lock was filled, and as I took the wheel, the upper lock gates swung open under the steamer's bow. Standing in the wheelhouse, fifty feet above the water, gave me a sense of superiority and freedom to look down on the people standing on the lock wall—only three or four lock employees now, for there are few sightseers around the locks in late November. Ice was appearing along the shore in the rivers. The thermometer stood at five above. The gale from the pole promised worse. It would be a wicked night on Superior.

I wondered what would happen to our deckload of new automobiles.

The lock gates were wide open now. Captain Breed blew one whistle blast and twisted the handle of the Chadburn to full ahead. The 610-foot *Selkirk* began to move. I watched her stern to keep her from swinging against the wall, keeping a turn of right wheel on her, for the gale of wind pressing on her starboard bow was wanting to blow the vessel sidewise. She finally cleared the end of the left-hand wall, passed the railroad bridge with its two black fingers sticking skyward on either side, and then there was more room as she thrust her nose past Vidal Shoal above the rapids. She steered badly, yawing in the crosswind.

Captain Breed spoke to the mate. "We'll need some more water in her, Chuck. Put some in the forepeak, too."

The mate took down the phone and called the engine room. Early darkness fell like a curtain when Point Iroquois was left astern. There was even a fair-sized sea rolling in Whitefish Bay, a sea that slammed and banged against the *Selkirk*'s bows, now and then throwing sheets of spray over the fo'c'sle that rapped like birdshot on the pilothouse windows. The skipper had the middle window almost shut, leaving a three-inch space open at the top to see through. You can't see through the spray steaming down the glass and freezing.

Isle Parisienne Light came abreast to starboard and fell astern. The storm outside worried at the freighter, seeming to shake her as a dog shakes a slipper. The roar and moan of the wind made conversation difficult. Captain Breed spoke above it. "Tell them to have the anchors ready, Chuck. We won't go outside tonight. Anchor under the point. Must be blowing fifty."

The mate went below to pass the order.

"You can left about ten degrees, Fred," Captain Breed said to me.

"Left ten degrees," I repeated and spun the wheel. I watched the gyro repeater click over, meeting her with a half-turn to the right as she came onto course. The skipper moved the Chadburn to half ahead. I gave her some more right wheel then, for I knew she would make greater leeway as she slowed. She was going along cornerwise, like a dog.

Dead ahead, in the heavy gloom, the flash of Whitefish

Point Light was intermittently blinding. It looked as though the ship would run the light down, though I knew, of course, that the light was several hundred yards back of the beach. Then, too, I was aware that because of the leeway she was making, the ship wouldn't fetch up anywhere near the light, even if we kept going that far, which naturally we wouldn't. But it gave me the creeps just the same—the wild night—and from that height the lighthouse looked mighty close.

The light was well to starboard now, when Captain Breed ordered, "Hard right, Fred. Head her right on the light again now." And the skipper rang the engine room for stop; then in another minute he swung the handle full astern. He stepped over and uncovered the speaking tube to the windlass room. "All right, Chuck, let go the starboard anchor." The vessel shuddered as the chain ran out the hawse pipe. The captain rang the engine-room telegraph to stop. Then he opened the window wide and shouted down to the watchman out on the fo'c'sle head, "How does she lead, Peter?"

"Straight ahead, sir."

The skipper rang for half speed ahead then as he ordered me to put her hard left. I spun the wheel over fast until the warning bell on the steering post gave out its small ping. "Hard over left, sir."

"Hard over left," Captain Breed repeated. He called out the window again, "How much chain have you got out there?"

"Ten fathoms."

Captain Breed rang the engines to stop and shouted in the speaking tube, "Let your other anchor go, Chuck." Then to me, "You can put her amidships now, Fred."

In a couple of minutes, the mate came up with the watchman. The wheelhouse was cold—I was shivering standing there at the wheel—and the skipper shut the window.

Captain Breed went below to turn in for the night, saying, "Call me if the wind shifts, Chuck."

For the rest of the watch, there was nothing to do but watch the ship swing at her anchors. She dragged for a time, and then the anchors held. With the sound of a great pipe organ, the gale fought the ship, running the scale from bass to treble and back with an obligato background, ever pressing on the consciousness. Eerily, the searching finger of the lighthouse beam swept the horizon, its white glare lighting up the pilothouse intermittently with midday brilliance.

She was still lying at anchor when I awakened next morning. The gale seemed scarcely lessened. Snow covered the deck and its load of automobiles as I made my way aft for breakfast. The temperature had fallen below zero, and the calm water along the shore in the lee of the point showed ice cover. Several other steamers were anchored nearby, all covered with the same winter frosting.

Half an hour after the mate and I had struggled forward to go on watch, the skipper appeared in the wheelhouse. Tall and spare, competent, intelligent, and with his ready grin, he was the perfect skipper for a fellow to sail with, though he looked more like a high school English teacher.

"The wind feels like it was letting up a little bit, Chuck," he ventured as he closed the door. "Damn cold, but the gale's easing off."

"Yes, sir, she's slacking some." The two were old friends in the line and understood each other. The mate practically worshipped the Old Man. I had a strong fondness for him myself.

"She's blowing fairly stiff yet," Captain Breed said, "but I think we can get up the hooks and get out of here."

"Would help if we had a weather report," the mate said.

"She'll take it all right," Captain Breed said. "Keep

164

plenty of water in her." He turned to the blackboard which showed the soundings from the last watch. "We could stand a bit more. Let's fill up the forepeak, eh? Put about ten or twelve feet in forward, and fill 'er up aft. We'll want to keep her wheel buried. Chief won't like it if she kicks her wheel out. Might tear herself to pieces. She's really rolling out there."

The ship-to-shore phone broke in with the weather report. The mate took the phone and dialed a channel. He wrote down a string of numbers.

"Northwest thirty-five in the first period, northeast fifteen in the second," he reported. "This is the last of it, I guess."

"All right, Chuck, let's get the hooks up." Captain Breed moved the handle on the Chadburn to stand by. The mate went below, and soon I could hear the anchor windlass rumbling. As the second anchor came up, the captain rang for full speed ahead and ordered me to put her hard right. We came around Whitefish Point in the trough of a heavy sea so that the ship rolled wildly several times before I got her around again and headed into it.

In the midst of that frightful rolling, I looked back for a moment at the deck load. The autos were chained down, and, save for a few bumped fenders, there was no particular damage.

It was an awe-inspiring sight outside the point. An endless procession of huge combers raced toward the vessel, at least three hundred feet long they were, crest to crest, and forty feet high, for they came over the railings regularly, and the railings were fifteen or twenty feet above the waterline.

The automobiles were taking a beating and icing up rapidly. We pitched and rolled like a rowboat. I found it hard to keep the steamer on course.

A couple of ship's lengths off to starboard, another

freighter, smaller than the *Selkirk* and loaded deep with coal, made heavy going of it. The skipper and the mate and I watched her as sea after sea mounted her fo'c'sle, smothering her pilothouse and completely blotting her forward end from sight.

"She can't take that long," Captain Breed said.

As he spoke, a bigger sea than the others smashed at the other steamer's bow. For a moment, we could see nothing forward but the upper half of her spar. She shook herself free of the deluge, her wheelhouse, cabins, and fo'c'sle emerging from the inundation as it swept aft along her deck and tore at her after house. Some of her hatch tarpaulins were torn loose. Another minute, and she was turning about. She came around slowly, ponderously, rolling her decks under on either side until it seemed she must roll completely over. But they got her about safely and headed back for shelter.

We heard later over the ship-to-shore telephone that the other ship had smashed in her pilothouse windows and that the great sea, as we watched, had torn her wheelsman away from the wheel and thrown him against the chart table, breaking his arm and several ribs.

The *Selkirk* wasn't having a picnic of it. All day, she slammed into the marching gray seas that tossed her bow skyward then dropped her into the hollows, booming and hammering against her forward end, lifting her anchors up into the hawse pipes and dropping them, filling the air with sheets of spray, and sometimes even rising green across the fo'c'sle bulwarks.

A strange sight was the automobiles covered with water and emerging again as the waves drained off. Two or three broke loose; the mates and the crew, at the risk of their lives, chained them down again. Frightfully cold work it was back there on the spar deck, in the icy water and zero weather.

Not one of us thought of going aft along that ice-coated deck at noon for dinner. We went without.

After a time, it wasn't necessary to tighten the chains, for the cars were all encased in ice and frozen solidly to the hatches.

I had turned in, hungry, to snatch some sleep, though it wasn't easy, what with the crazy motion of the ship. I had a dream of being in downtown traffic in a large city. When I woke up, I thought I was still dreaming, for I heard the blowing of automobile horns, persistently. And then another, and another. A crazy sound, the like of which I'd never heard before. The freighter was still tossing and rolling.

Looking out the porthole aft along the deck, I saw the mate and the deck watch attacking a car with axes, chopping away the ice. The mate ripped open the hood of one of the autos and reached inside. Then I realized what was happening. The ice had shorted the horns on the cars, and the only way they could stop the noise was to rip the wires loose. I lay back in my bunk and howled. I guess there must have been fifty horns all blowing at once.

Mr. Ford would have liked that story, if we could have talked.

FATHERS AND SONS

If Mr. Ford and I could have talked, we might have talked about sons and grandsons, too. I mean, Mr. Ford must have been proud that his grandson followed him in his line of work . . . to name a boat for him.

I was hoping my own son would follow my line of work.

The United States was at war. Lake shipping was flowing at a volume never before equaled. New freighters were being built at shipyards, men were scarce, and vessels frequently had to leave port without a full crew. Though I had given up the lakes for a career ashore, I had been drawn back by their undying lure and had shipped out with my old friend Captain Jacobsen.

My eighteen-year-old son, Ted, had finished high school and was waiting for a call from the Air Force, in which he had enlisted a few months earlier. The *Hutchinson* was in Cleveland unloading ore at the C.&P. dock, and the boy had driven in to see his father and look over the fine new ship. Visiting on deck, we talked of the ship, and Ted was wishing he could sail with his father, when Captain Jacobsen came down the companionway from his quarters. I introduced the boy to the skipper, and the young man voiced his desire to sail with the ship.

"Have you got a seaman's book?" the captain asked him.

"Yes, sir."

"All right, you're hired." And the captain walked aft.

Ted went home and packed and returned to the ship, where he was signed on as a deckhand. The freighter sailed at midnight.

It was a good moment for us both. We had never sailed together on the same ship before, except as passengers when he was a small boy.

The next morning found the *Hutchinson* plowing up the Detroit River past Detroit, the river sparkling in the sunlight, Belle Isle on the port side—a lovely summer morning giving promise of a grand trip ahead. I had the four-to-eight watch at the wheel, and when I came forward from breakfast later, Ted and I sat in the lee of the fo'c'sle, getting the heat out of the weak sunlight. Then the boy had some duties to occupy him for an hour. When he returned, he said, "Guess what I just heard over the ship-to-shore phone?"

"Something about the war?"

"No, Dad, I just heard that your son has to report to Fort Thomas, Kentucky, in five days." And he had a queer, hurt grin on his face.

It took a while for the news to sink in, then it dawned on me. "Why, dammit, that means you can't even finish this trip."

"That's right."

"Well, I'll be damned." I thought for a few minutes. What could we do? The trip would take six days, and it was necessary for him to be back home in four. I became conscious of a terrible feeling of loneliness.

We finally consulted the captain, but there was no solution other than that Ted should leave the ship at Port Huron, five hours ahead. Captain Jacobsen was most sympathetic, and he went to the trouble of paying off the young man for a day's work.

The hours went by all too fast as the *Hutch* snored on up the St. Clair River. I sat in my room with Ted. He was a little sad, a little frightened, lounging in his father's berth. There was hardly anything to say. Here he had his first chance to sail with his dad, and after fifteen hours he had to leave for camp.

Neither of us voiced what was really in our minds: Would we ever see each other again? Ted had elected to be a pilot in the most frightful war the world had ever put on. We both tried to be cheerful, but . . .

Marysville was abreast now—a few more minutes.

"Guess we better go on deck now, Ted."

"Yup."

The little speedboat was coming out from Port Huron.

The great freighter slackened speed and hung a bos'n's ladder over the side. A heaving line dropped to the speedboat and was made fast. Our hands gripped for a moment, then Ted went over the side.

"Good-bye, Dad."

"So long. Take care of yourself."

The speedboat sheered away for the shore.

I made my way to the pilothouse to take the wheel.

The following afternoon I climbed to the pilothouse to go on watch. Repeating the course given me by the other wheelsman, I noted a great disarray of papers all over the chart table. The skipper was calling figures to the first mate, who was punching them into an adding machine. After a time, I was drawn into the work. The payroll was out of balance in the amount of $2.55. After the skipper went below, I tried it a couple of times [the ship was steering herself by the iron mike] and finally caught on to the fact that a deckhand had been paid $2.55 too much. The mate called the captain about it, and everyone went back to navigating the ship. I balanced the books by putting up the $2.55 out of my pocket, which satisfied everyone around, for it was Ted who had been overpaid.

In all these decades of steamboating, strangely (or maybe everybody's that way), I continued thinking of myself as a young man on the way up. Always looking ahead, not behind me. I apparently never noticed the gradual influx of young seamen coming aboard behind me. Didn't notice that now there were more men aboard who were younger than I than men who were older.

Two events woke me up. One day, I casually asked one of the new men to give me a hand at the ladder with my duffel. Usually a fellow would answer, "Sure." But this young fellow, in all sincerity and with much alacrity, said, "Sure, sir!"

It gave me pause.

The second event came when I shipped out one fall on one of the "super dupers"—which were the largest and most modern vessels on the lakes, 639 feet long with a 70-foot beam and a cargo capacity of 18,000 tons. Driven by turbines, they were fast as lake ships go, having a speed, loaded, of some thirteen miles per hour. The ship was equipped with electric hatch cranes, electric winches with controls at the railings, electric gyro-compass and gyro-pilot, and all the other latest navigating devices. Proud ships and beautiful, they made a round trip from Duluth or Two Harbors to Conneaut and back in five days or a little more. But that was a drawback, for there was little time to go ashore at either end of the trip. It was like riding a ferryboat, almost, and rather monotonous after a time.

Still, they had a lot of power and steered well and easily. But the engine room was a disappointment to me. I always liked to go down and watch the engines work. Turbines have no visible moving parts. They look for all the world like great tanks. The only thing that seems to be moving is the tail shaft. The pumps are driven by turbines that are enclosed, as are the dynamos. An interesting place in the eyes of the young men aboard, but I found it boring.

It was impossible, too, to visit with the engineers, for these drab-looking turbines gave off a continual high-pitched screaming which hardly left room for thought.

So I didn't often visit the engine room anymore. It was more interesting in the pilothouse.

And yet even the pilothouse had instruments now and apparatus that took a lot of the suspense out of sailing. There was a time this new gadgetry would have made me marvel.

George A. Sloan. (Alan W. Sweigert photo.)

But I found myself instead marveling at mates I'd known who had to do with a pencil what some of these gadgets did—had to know down to a point as fine as frog's hair their wind and drift and whether she's loaded by the head or stern and how much water she's got in her, and be able to do everything by hand or they'd lose their tickets. *These were sailors!*

And when you get into that kind of way of thinking, a fellow starts to ask himself . . . if it's time to go ashore.

Titles in the Great Lakes Books Series

Let the Drum Beat: A History of the Detroit Light Guard, by Stanley D. Solvick, 1988

Over the Graves of Horses, by Michael Delp, 1988

Wolf in Sheep's Clothing: The Search for a Child Killer, by Tommy McIntyre, 1988

Artists in Michigan, 1900–1976: A Biographical Dictionary, introduction by Dennis Barrie, biographies by Jeanie Huntley Bentley, Cynthia Newman Helms, and Mary Chris Rospond, 1989

Copper-Toed Boots, by Marguerite de Angeli, 1989 (reprint)

Deep Woods Frontier: A History of Logging in Northern Michigan, by Theodore J. Karamanski, 1989

Detroit: City of Race and Class Violence, revised edition, by B. J. Widick, 1989

Detroit Images: Photographs of the Renaissance City, edited by John J. Bukowczyk and Douglas Aikenhead, with Peter Slavcheff, 1989

Hangdog Reef: Poems Sailing the Great Lakes, by Stephen Tudor, 1989

Orvie, The Dictator of Dearborn, by David L. Good, 1989

America's Favorite Homes: A Guide to Popular Early Twentieth-Century Homes, by Robert Schweitzer and Michael W. R. Davis, 1990

Beyond the Model T: The Other Ventures of Henry Ford, by Ford R. Bryan, 1990

Detroit Kids Catalog: The Hometown Tourist, by Ellyce Field, 1990

Detroit Perspectives: Crossroads and Turning Points, edited by Wilma Henrickson, 1990

The Diary of Bishop Frederic Baraga: First Bishop of Marquette, Michigan, edited by Regis M. Walling and Rev. N. Daniel Rupp, 1990

Life after the Line, by Josie Kearns, 1990

The Making of Michigan, 1820–1860: A Pioneer Anthology, edited by Justin L. Kestenbaum, 1990

Michigan Lumbertowns: Lumbermen and Laborers in Saginaw, Bay City, and Muskegon, 1870–1905, by Jeremy W. Kilar, 1990

The Pottery of John Foster: Form and Meaning, by Gordon and Elizabeth Orear, 1990

Seasons of Grace: A History of the Catholic Archdiocese of Detroit, by Leslie Woodcock Tentler, 1990

Waiting for the News, by Leo Litwak, 1990 (reprint)

Walnut Pickles and Watermelon Cake: A Century of Michigan Cooking, by Larry B. Massie and Priscilla Massie, 1990

John Jacob Astor: Business and Finance in the Early Republic, by John Haeger, 1991

Life on the Great Lakes: A Wheelsman's Story, by Fred W. Dutton, edited by William Donohue Ellis, 1991

Steamboats and Sailors of the Great Lakes, by Mark L. Thompson, 1991

Survival and Regeneration: Detroit's American Indian Community, by Edmund J. Danziger, Jr., 1991